THE MAPLE SYRUP COOKBOOK

THE MAPLE SYRUP COOKBOOK

by
Ken Haedrich

For my parents

A Garden Way Publishing Book

Storey Communications, Inc.
Schoolhouse Road
Pownal, Vermont 05261

Cover design by Wanda Harper
Cover photograph by Rudi Legname
Illustrations by Anna Rich © 1988
Production and design by Wanda Harper
Edited by Andrea Chesman
Typeset by Accura Type & Design, Barre, Vermont, in Bookman.

Cover photo copyright © 1987 Bon Appetit Publishing Corp. Used with permission.

The name Garden Way Publishing is licenced to Storey Communications, Inc. by Garden Way, Inc.

Printed in the United States by Capital City Press
Third printing, February 1992

Library of Congress Cataloging-in-Publication Data

Haedrich, Ken, 1954-
  The maple syrup cookbook.

  "A Garden Way Publishing book."
  Includes index.
  1. Cookery (Maple sugar and syrup) 2. Maple
syrup. I. Title.
TX767.M3H34 1989   641.6'36   88-45485
ISBN 0-88233-524-3
ISBN 0-88233-524-5 (pbk.)

Contents

Foreword

In the traditions of the past, Ken Haedrich and I would be exchanging recipes over the back fence, as good friends and neighbors used to do. And judging from the recipes Ken has gathered here in *The Maple Syrup Cookbook*, a gratifying exchange it would have been.

Instead of over the back fence, Ken and I have had our kitchen talks over the phone for many years now. And we've exchanged our share of letters. In addition, I've followed his cooking column in *Country Journal* magazine, as well as the recipes and articles he has published elsewhere. Through it all, I've come to know Ken as a fine, American home cook who has great enthusiasm and a respect for simple, wholesome ingredients — an attitude that stands out clearly in his writing and recipes.

Recently, I visited Ken for the first time at his home in the quiet woods of New Hampshire, where he lives with his young family. When I sat down in Ken's kitchen and ate his good warm biscuits and pies — including several of the ones you'll find here — it was just the kind of homey visit with a friend that we all love.

With any luck, I'll be back to visit Ken soon. But in the meantime, if I can't eat his own good maple pies, cakes, cookies, and breakfasts, I can at least keep a copy of *The Maple Syrup Cookbook* close by, to make them for myself.

It seems most appropriate that Ken, with his fondness for pure and simple ingredients, should write this maple syrup cookbook. Maple syrup is one of America's most delicious natural foods, and Ken has done a good job of giving us recipes that let the wonderful flavor of maple syrup come through.

Marion Cunningham

Preface

This book, and its less ambitious predecessor I self-published several years ago, came about for a rather modest reason. It was not intended to fan the reported flames of interest in American cookery or Native American ingredients (though I would not be disappointed if it did so). Nor did it grow out of any unswerving commitment to healthy or natural foods; heaven knows, I can claim any number of food preferences that aren't likely to add years to my life. And besides, as natural a food as maple syrup may be, the word natural has been so exploited in food advertising that it ceases to have any clear meaning anymore.

Yes, as much as I could have been motivated to write a maple syrup cookbook for a variety of honorable intentions, the reason I did is simply because I love the stuff in a big way. I love the flavor, the smell, and the color of pure maple syrup, a combination of sensual pleasures nobody has been able to capture with artificial ingredients. Real maple syrup is so special that its very presence in a dish or at a meal inspires awe and grabs attention. Serve it on pancakes, drizzle it on ice cream, sweeten a cheesecake with it and people take note, feel honored, as though a visiting dignitary had joined them for the meal. That's the magic quality I love about maple syrup.

Having lived and cooked in one capacity or another here in New Hampshire for the last ten years, I've had ample opportunity to experiment with pure maple syrup, to discover for myself where maple seems to work best in cooking. In addition, I've met a number of sugarmakers, professional cooks, and talented home cooks too, many of whom are as passionate about maple syrup as I am. Not only has meeting these people deepened my admiration for maple — the natural result of getting to know the maple syrup producers themselves — but it has also shed outside light on my maple syrup cooking and steered me toward a repertoire of maple syrup recipes I think reflects the ways cooks most enjoy using maple syrup in the kitchen.

That's what this cookbook is all about — enjoyable ways to use maple syrup in the kitchen.

Rather than try too hard here for an evenhanded distribution of recipes — entrées, salads, dressings, desserts, and so forth — I decided to more or less let the material seek its own natural balance. Thus, you'll see that the sweets far outweigh the savory applications of maple syrup. That's to be expected. The hefty breakfast section of this book should come as no surprise either. Maple syrup has an unabashed partiality toward breakfast, a bias you'll see I've indulged with a satisfying assortment of pancakes, waffles, fruit dishes, breakfast breads, and more.

Here's hoping that all of the maple syrup recipes in this book, as well as any of your own adaptations they might inspire, give you and your loved ones as much pleasure as they have me and mine.

Maple Syrup
Savvy

Though it is widely believed that the Indians were experienced sugarmakers long before the white man arrived in North America, when and how they learned to make maple syrup is a mystery. An Indian legend has it that there was once a time when sap issued from the maple tree in a near-pure syrup form, something that a formidable god by the name of Ne-naw-Bo-zhoo decided to bring to a halt. Anticipating, no doubt correctly, that syrup thus had would be too easily taken for granted, he diluted it with water. Sugarmakers have been boiling the water out of sap ever since, in the pursuit of pure maple syrup.

There is, in fact, a certain amount of disagreement among food historians as to just how adept the Indians could have been at making maple products. In their fascinating book, *The Maple Sugar Book*, Helen and Scott Nearing quickly put to rest the notion, found elsewhere, that the Indians did not tap maples or make syrup until the Europeans came and taught them how. "Can it be," a Kickapoo chief is said to have snapped at a traveler who dared to raise the issue, "that thou art so simple as to ask me such a question, seeing that the Master of Life has imparted to us an instinct which enabled us to substitute stone hatchets and knives for those made of steel by the whites; wherefore should we not have known as well as they how to manufacture sugar?"

Legend has designated the first maple syrup maker and cook as an Iroquois squaw, the wife of one Chief Woksis. One late winter morning, the story goes, the chief headed out on one of his hunts, but not before yanking his tomahawk from the tree where he'd thrown it the night before. On this particular day the weather turned quite warm, causing the tree's sap to run and fill a container standing near the trunk. The squaw spied the vessel and, thinking it was plain water, cooked her evening meal in it. The boiling that ensued turned the sap to syrup, flavoring the chief's meal as never before. And thus began the tradition of making maple syrup.

The Indians are likely to have converted most of their maple syrup to maple sugar. Liquid storage vessels were few and maple sugar was far easier to store and transport. They put their "Indian sugar" into specially made birch bark boxes known as *mokuks*, and carried containers of it to market. Along with these larger blocks of maple sugar, which they sold or traded, the Indians made molded sugar candies. The molds were, as one observer noted, "cut from soft wood and greased before the sirup was put into them so that it could easily be taken out. These molds were in shapes of various animals, also of men, and of the moon and stars, originality being sought."

The Indians were anything but timid in their exploration of a syrup-based cuisine. The northeastern Indians had never learned to make salt from seawater, and even after the settlers came and salt became available, the Indians never embraced it. So maple syrup or sugar went in, or on, almost everything. They cooked fish and meats in maple water. Maple went into their basic gruel and in little cakes made from ground corn mixed with chestnuts, beans, and berries. James Smith, in his account of life with the Indians during the mid-1700s, wrote that "we commonly used our [maple] sugar while encamped by putting it in bear's fat until the fat was almost as sweet as the sugar itself, and in this we dipped our roasted venison."

The arrival of our early settlers brought the white man's innovations to the sugarmaker's art. Foremost among these were iron and copper kettles, which proved to be far less perishable than the wooden and clay troughs used by the Indians for boiling sap. The white man realized that the Indian way of tapping maples — by cutting deep gashes into the bark — not only wasted sap but injured the trees. So he took to drilling tapholes with an auger.

Collection methods were further improved by the settlers when they replaced the Indians' birch bark containers with more reliable ones fashioned from ash or basswood trees. The large trunk sections of these trees were cut to length, halved, and then hollowed out into crude troughs. Over time, these clumsy troughs were replaced by buckets and, finally, by hanging buckets, hung by metal spikes. The spikes are long since history, of course, because modern taps are made to support the weight of the bucket or tubing. But even now, much to the sawer's dismay, one will show up deeply embedded in a maple being cut into lumber.

The Indian way of boiling sap was to drop red hot stones into wooden dugout troughs where the sap was held. And weather permitting, they would also remove water from sap by freezing instead of boiling. The water would rise to the top of the troughs and freeze, leaving unfrozen, concentrated sap below. The large cauldrons brought by the settlers were more efficient for boiling than the wooden troughs. With the kettle method of boiling, a large cauldron was suspended over a blazing fire, supported by a pole frame. Sometimes, a series of kettles was used, and the sugarmakers ladled the partially evaporated sap from one kettle to the next. In this way, syrup could be made on a continuous basis instead of, as one participant wrote, boiling "the same sap from morning till night by constantly replenishing the kettle, thus wasting time and fuel and sacrificing quality."

When you stop to consider the laborious nature of sugarmaking against the already rigorous backdrop of pioneer life, you might wonder why the early settlers even bothered. Were there no alternatives?

There were, actually — honey,

for one. In fact, honey bees had been imported from Italy as early as 1630. But beekeepers were few in the colonies and honey was relatively rare, and would remain so for years to come.

Molasses, on the other hand, was abundant and soon began arriving from West Indian sugar plantations. (Sugar itself, of which molasses is a by-product, was still prohibitively expensive.) But molasses was a thorn in the side of the settlers, not just for the high cost of transporting it from the coast by pack horse, but also because the molasses trade supported slavery in the most direct way. "Make your own sugar," advised the *Farmer's Almanac* in 1803, "and send not to the Indies for it. Feast not on the toil, pain and misery of the wretched."

This passage from the Nearings' book, in a letter from Benjamin Rush to Thomas Jefferson, perhaps best illustrates what maple products represented to the strongly antislavery colonists: "I cannot help contemplating a Sugar Maple Tree with a species of affection, and even veneration; for I have persuaded myself to behold in it the happy means of rendering the commerce and slavery of our African brethren in the sugar islands, as unnecessary as it has always been inhuman and unjust. I shall conclude this letter by wishing that the patronage which you have afforded to the Maple Sugar, as well as the Maple Tree, by your example [Mr. Jefferson is purported to have used no other sugar in his family than maple and to have planted an orchard of maples on his farm in Virginia] may produce an influence in our country as extensive as your reputation for useful science and genuine patriotism."

Today, of course, maple products account for but a small fraction of the sweetener used in this country. Only one hundred years ago, however — at least in the northeastern part of the United States — maple ranked first. Whereas a century ago, 90 percent of the maple crop was converted to maple sugar, today only a small amount is, since most consumers buy maple primarily for pancakes and waffles. Nonetheless, maple syrup, as more cooks are discovering every year, can indeed play a leading role in the modern kitchen.

How Maple Syrup Is Made

In some respects, very little about the process of making maple syrup has changed since the first sugarmakers of record, the North American Indians. Today, of course, sugarmakers have at their disposal a number of time-saving and labor-saving innovations, from plastic tubing to reverse osmosis machines. But these inroads only hasten the transition from sap to syrup; in no way do they diminish maple's magic. The flavor, quality, and wholesome goodness of maple syrup, if anything, have improved over the years. And in an age when so many of our comestibles have been reduced to nothing more than machine-made synthetics, maple syrup remains an oasis of purity, still made on the farm by men and women whose connection with the earth is part of their daily lives.

Maple syrup is produced in

the northeastern part of the United States, the upper Midwest, and in adjacent sections of Canada, covering a select area from Maine, as far south as West Virginia, and west to Minnesota. Though the range of *acer saccharum* and *acer nigrum*, the two principal sugar maples, extends beyond this area, the unique combination of altitude, soil conditions, and weather patterns necessary for maple syrup production — freezing nights followed by warming, above-freezing days — does not, much to the chagrin, one suspects, of the Europeans, who have tried without success to manufacture maple syrup on their own turf.

Maple sap is a clear liquid containing nutrients from the soil and organic substances manufactured by the leaves. It tastes somewhat sweet, with a sugar content on the average of 2 to 3 percent, though the percentage can run as high as 6 percent, varying from tree to tree, from sugar bush to sugar bush, from one week to the next, and from one year to the next. The sugar in the maple sap is synthesized by the leaves and stored in the tree as starch. This starch is the food of the plant, and in the fall and spring, with the further action of sunlight, it is converted into sucrose and in turn to invert sugar.

Sugaring season begins as early as January and often extends well into April. The Indians, for whom this was a season of celebration, referred to this period as "the sugar moon." Sap does not flow in freezing weather, but as the warmish days of late winter return, the sap begins to move with vigor and sugarmakers set out their taps.

Tapholes are usually bored 2 to 2½ inches deep, with a 7/16-inch bit. A bit and brace are sometimes used, but more common today is the automatic drill. Tapholes are drilled on a slight downward path to facilitate the flow of sap, and they are located anywhere from about 3 to 5 feet off the ground. Not just any sugar maple can, or should, be tapped. Those trees, for instance, yielding a sap with a sugar content of 1 percent are not considered economically worth the trouble because of their low syrup yields, and are therefore often culled.

Opinions vary, but conventional wisdom maintains that trees selected for tapping should have a minimum diameter of 12 inches, 4½ feet from the ground. As the diameter increases, so may the number of taps, at the rate of one tap for each 10-inch increase. Since tapping a maple subjects the tree to a certain amount of stress, many experienced sugarmakers strongly recommend not exceeding 3 taps per tree, no matter how large it is.

There's no dearth of down-home wisdom regarding the placement of taps — "the higher (or lower) the tap, the sweeter the sap"; "tap the warm side of the tree"; "the older the tree, the sweeter the sap" — but studies have shown that tap location has little or no appreciable effect on yield. With each successive year, the position of new tapholes is staggered, to avoid hitting old tapholes or dead tissue hidden by new bark, which may contribute to reduced sap flow.

Into every taphole a spout or spile is driven. All spouts have a tapered "shoulder" — the part that goes into the tree — in order to form a tight, leakproof seal with the bark and outer sapwood. Through the spout the sap flows, either into a sap bucket hung directly on the spout or into plastic tubing.

Sap buckets in one form or another have been used in the collection of maple sap for some 300 years. One early observer of the Indians describes their sap buckets, which were "fashioned from birchbark, cut and folded at the corners...and seamed with pine resin. The buckets were of various sizes, though usually held from 1 to 2 gallons."

The standard sap bucket today is a 15-quart, galvanized metal container. It has a cover to keep out rain and assorted detritus. Sap buckets are emptied by hand and poured into a central, and usually portable, collection tank. Manual sap collection is a slow, labor-intensive activity and accounts, according to one source, for as much as one-third of the cost of syrup production.

The advent of plastic tubing has dramatically changed sap collection methods, and most large maple operations have made the switch from buckets to tubing. Tubing is not the perfect solution — squirrels nibble on it, moose trample through it, tree limbs fall on it, and careful cleaning is required. But plastic tubing has eliminated much of the drudgery associated with manual sap collection. With tubing, one no longer needs to build roads or paths, often through inhospitable terrain, to gather sap. Tubing is light and easy to carry. And it allows for a continuous flow of sap to the sugarhouse or roadside storage tanks.

Whether collected by bucket or fed by plastic tubing, all sap eventually finds its way to the sugarhouse, there to be boiled down to syrup. The typical modern sugarhouse is apt to have one or more large sap storage tanks, a wood-fired or oil-fired evaporator for boiling the sap, a finishing pan for completing the boiling, some type of filtering system, bulk storage barrels for storing the finished syrup, and a storage area for packaged syrup. Depending on the sophistication of the opera-tion, you may also find a reverse osmosis machine — which removes up to 60 percent of the water content before the sap reaches the evaporator — and a specially equipped kitchen for the manufacture of maple sugar candies.

The backbone of the sugarhouse is the evaporator, essentially a large pan used for boiling water from the sap. Evaporators have come a long way since the wooden troughs used by the Indians. The modern evaporator was introduced in about 1900, and its advantages over its flat-bottomed predecessor were significant. Flues beneath the pan not only trap heat and increase fuel efficiency, but they provide a greater heating surface, and therefore increase the rate of evaporation.

The typical evaporator is a two-pan affair, supported by a heavy metal frame called an arch. From the storage tanks, the sap enters the sap or back pan, the larger of the two pans, where the boiling process begins. Great plumes of steam soon rise from the evaporator as the water is boiled out of the sap. Many evaporators have a hood directly over the sap pan, enclosing a bank of pipes where incoming sap is preheated, which further speeds up the rate of evaporation.

Concentrated sap flows down the back pan and enters by a connecting pipe into the front or syrup pan, located over the firebox. The syrup pan is where the final or near-final stage of boiling takes place. As it gets closer and closer to finished density, the sap in the syrup pan moves through a series of baffles toward a drawoff valve. The purpose of the baffles is to guard against the constant intermixing of saps of different densities, so syrup can be drawn off on a continuous basis, instead of in one large batch. The result is higher grade yields of syrup.

Experienced sugarmakers can tell by sight — judging by the color and the look of the bubbles in the syrup pan — when the syrup is ready to be drawn off. They'll dip a paddle or scoop into the pan, lift it up and check to see if the syrup "sheets" or "aprons" off the paddle in the fashion that indicates the syrup

point has been reached. The precise tests for doneness, however, are based on readings from precision instruments.

Sap becomes syrup at 7 to 7.1 degrees above the boiling point of water. At sea level, water will boil at 212° F. But for every 550-foot increase in elevation, the boiling point drops by 1 degree. The correct temperature at which sap becomes syrup, therefore, varies with the location of the sugarhouse, and to some degree with barometric pressure, which can also affect the exact boiling point. With late winter weather conditions in maple country anything but stable — Mark Twain once commented that if you don't like our weather here in New England, just wait a minute — sugarmakers will regularly recheck the boiling point, even within the same day.

While an accurate temperature reading is an important guide to finished syrup, maple syrup produced for sale must be checked for proper density with a hydrometer. At room temperature, standard density of syrup is 66.5 to 66.7° Brix, the scale sugarmakers use for measuring

the percentage of sugar in syrup. A precise reading is important. Syrup with a density just a little below this range will taste thin and watery. A little above, and the syrup runs the risk of becoming crystallized in storage. Because this finishing of syrup to just the right density is such an important step in the making of syrup, many sugarmakers transfer near-syrup to a special finishing pan, where this step can be carefully controlled, instead of completing the boiling in the evaporator.

Once the syrup has been filtered to remove impurities, it is graded and hot-packed to prevent the growth of mold. Syrup is packaged by liquid measure into standard size containers, usually made of plastic or metal. The maple syrup, which by now has been reduced from as much as 40 parts of sap, is now ready for grading and sale.

Grading

Though grading is not mandatory in all states, much of the maple syrup sold over the counter in this country is assigned a grade. Grade is determined to a large extent by color, but also by flavor. Some of the factors that account for grade are the sugar content of the sap, how quickly — and at what point in the season — it was collected and boiled, and the rate of evaporation.

A certain amount of confusion exists in regard to grading. This stems from the fact that grading terms have changed over the years. In addition, even though there are United States standards, some states have adopted their own grading language. Basically, however, the system looks something like this:

US Grade A Light Amber. Light amber syrup, called "Fancy syrup" in Vermont, is regarded as the best tasting and highest grade of syrup available. It's generally the most expensive. Light amber has what's known in the maple industry as a "maple bouquet," or a very delicate but clear maple flavor. Light amber syrup is generally made in the beginning of the syrup season, because early season temperatures are normally lower and

there's less chance of sap fermentation — one of the factors that contribute to dark, lower grade syrup.

US Grade A Medium Amber. Medium amber syrup is, obviously, darker in color than light amber and has a pronounced maple flavor. It is considered a good all-purpose syrup, because it is delicate enough to be used with subtle flavors — such as ice cream, fruit, in whipped cream — but is generally used more as a table syrup than for cooking and baking.

US Grade A Dark Amber. Dark amber syrup has a deep color and a strong flavor, characterized by some as "caramel-like." Some people find it too assertive to be used as a table syrup, on pancakes, waffles, and the like. For practical purposes, however, it is no less adaptable than medium amber syrup.

US Grade B. Also called Grade C in Vermont, this is a very dark, intensely flavored syrup recommended primarily for baking. It's the least expen-

sive grade of syrup sold over the counter.

Canadian Grades. Under the Canadian grading system, the top three grades fall under the category called Canada #1. They are: Canada Extra Light, Canada Light, and Canada Medium. The Canadian system, however, breaks what we call Grade B — where there can be discernible variations in syrup quality —into two separate categories: Canada #2 — Amber — and Canada #3 — Dark.

If I were to translate all of this grading into some practicable buying guidelines or suggestions for the cook, basically I'd say don't be too concerned about grades. Don't ignore the grade, because it will give you a clue as to the syrup's flavor and intensity. But the only way you'll ever find out just which grade you prefer for a particular use is to try a number of them. Let your tastebuds and your pocketbook be your guides. Just because a certain grade is supposedly best for cooking or baking doesn't mean you won't enjoy it on pancakes. Taste is a very individual matter.

Maple Syrup: The Real Thing

Maple syrup is syrup made by the evaporation of maple sap or by the solution of maple sugar, and contains not more than approximately 33 to 35 percent water. That, by definition, is The Real Thing.

Then, of course, there's the imitation maple syrup, sometimes called pancake syrup, that is sold by several national food companies. Imitation maple syrup is mostly corn syrup and perhaps contains 2 or 3 percent of The Real Thing. For the purposes of this book, when we say maple syrup we're referring to pure, genuine, 100 percent maple syrup. If there is any question in your mind whether you are buying real or imitation syrup, read the packaging carefully. And if necessary, check with the store manager.

If real maple syrup is indeed nothing more than 100 percent boiled sap, some substances may find their way into the finished product. Generally, these substances are found only in trace amounts and are the result of standard maple syrup production practices. In all likelihood you'd never be aware of their presence. Rarely, very rarely, have producers been found to intentionally adulterate their maple syrup with corn syrup or other liquid sugars, but it has happened. No reputable producer would ever dream of doing such a thing, but if you do suspect the syrup you've bought has been adulterated, you should contact the department of agriculture in the state where your syrup was purchased.

One of the more common residues found in maple syrup comes from defoamers. Defoamers can be one of several kinds of fat — butter, cream, vegetable oil, and so on —which sugarmakers use to break the surface tension of the bubble network that periodically rises to the top of the evaporator. By breaking the surface tension, the bubbles recede, rather than spill out onto the sugarhouse floor.

Yet another additive sometimes detected in maple syrup is formaldehyde, from paraformaldehyde tablets some producers put in tapholes. Paraformaldehyde tablets first became commercially available in the early sixties. The purpose of the tablets is, essentially, to delay the tree's natural healing of the taphole, thereby extending the period during which sap can flow. As the sap flows from the tree, only a trace amount of formaldehyde — less than 5 parts per million — dissolves into the sap, and most of that is removed in the boiling process.

While these trace amounts of formaldehyde are considered acceptable to the Food and Drug Administration, and — according to the FDA — constitute no human health risk, there is growing concern among sugarmakers about its use due to the adverse affects these pellets have had on maple trees. Much damage has been documented, and as a result many sugarmakers have eliminated their use altogether. Vermont, in fact, has outlawed these tablets. As a consumer, you should inquire from the source if you want assurance that the syrup you're buying is formaldehyde-free.

Storing Maple Syrup

I've never encountered storage problems with maple syrup, simply because it doesn't last very long around here. Generally speaking, however, syrup will keep best if it is transferred to clear, glass containers and kept cold. Freezing is the smartest option for long-term storage, one especially worth considering if your refrigerator space is limited. I know one woman who divides her occasional gallon purchase of syrup among 4 glass quart jars, leaving plenty of headspace for expansion of the syrup as it freezes, and freezing all but one. Then, when her refrigerator supply runs out, she takes another quart out of freezer storage.

Over time, you may find mold growing on your syrup in the refrigerator. Don't throw it away. Rather, strain it through cheesecloth and then bring the syrup to a boil. Pour it back into a clean container and your syrup will be almost as good as new and perfectly safe to use.

Also, if your syrup should crystallize, it can be restored to its liquid state by placing the container in a pan of very hot water.

Substitution Suggestions

Even with these recipes as your guide to maple syrup cooking and baking, sooner or later you may reach a point where you would like to strike out on your own. Perhaps you want to convert an old family favorite cookie recipe, or adapt something you find in a new cookbook. How should you proceed?

Well, that all depends. Some recipes are easier to convert than others. A recipe that will end up in liquid form — say a sauce or beverage — is seldom a problem because the texture isn't likely to be too critical. Some cakes, on the other hand, have a very precise balance of liquid to dry ingredients and they can be difficult to get just right. Then, you also have to factor in that maple syrup not only adds a brownish tinge to whatever it is you're cooking, but it tends to make baked goods brown more quickly than

sugar does. Do you want that and is it appropriate for what you're cooking?

Basically, you have to account for two things when substituting maple syrup for sugar in a recipe: that syrup is sweeter than sugar, and that it adds extra moisture to the recipe. Thus, the rule of thumb goes like this:

For general cooking, use only three-fourths the amount of maple syrup as sugar in a recipe. For example, if a recipe says to use 1/4 cup (4 tablespoons) sugar, use 3 tablespoons of maple syrup instead.

In baking, for every cup of sugar, substitute 3/4 cup maple syrup, and reduce the dominant liquid in the recipe by 3 tablespoons. By dominant I mean don't cut back on a liquid that is likely to alter the flavor or texture of a recipe, such as the liqueur, oil, or egg when you have 2 cups of milk to play with.

If you are serious about getting a recipe just right, measure your ingredients carefully and make notes where you've altered the recipe. Then, using your notes, try the recipe a second time if it doesn't work out as hoped, making the appropriate changes. Read the entire recipe through carefully, before you begin, and see how it makes sense to proceed.

And as far as substituting maple syrup for honey, I've found you can almost always succeed with an equivalent substitution.

Breakfast

In which we take a leisurely tour of crisp waffles,
towering stacks of pancakes, and
meet a sandwich called a Canadian Bacon
Cheese Dream

Pancakes and Waffles: Some Observations

For all of their apparent simplicity, making good pancakes is an acquired skill. Murphy's Law applies, and things do go wrong. This point was brought home to me not long ago when I developed a number of pancake recipes for a food magazine — recipes I had tested to death in my home kitchen —only to hear back from their test kitchen that several of the recipes hadn't worked for them. In the end we worked out the bugs, and in the process I learned that foolproof pancake-making hinges on several important, basic understandings. Let's briefly look at some of these variables.

The Batter. First and foremost, don't beat it. When you beat batter you develop the gluten, a wheat protein responsible for the formation of elastic strands, which in turn toughens your pancakes and keeps them from achieving a light, fluffy texture. So just stir your liquids into the dry ingredients until they're blended. The best tool I've found for this is a simple wire whisk with widely spaced strands. A wooden spoon or spatula work fine, too.

Even though pancake recipes always give precise measurements for ingredients, it is quite common for the batter to need adjusting. Generally it's in the direction of needing to be thinned, and this is especially true with whole grains, since they absorb moisture gradually as the batter sits around. After you've made a pancake recipe a number of times, you will learn the precise consistency and the pancake texture it will yield. Most pancake batters perform best when they are neither so thin they run all over creation, nor so thick you have to spread them around. I've found that my electric griddle produces better results with a slightly thicker batter, while my skillet works best with a thinner batter.

The Cooking Surface. Basically, the more metal you can put between your heat source and your pancakes, the better. A thick, heavy surface spreads the heat around, and the pancakes cook evenly, whereas a thin pan cooks spottily and you get "hot spots" on your pancakes. Cast iron is really superb. I have a special cast-iron pancake skillet, which I use only for pancakes and warming tortillas. It has very low sides, so I can slide the spatula under the pancakes easily. The pan has a glossy black seasoning built on by years of use. The seasoning acts as a sort of natural, nonstick finish, so I'm careful not to scrub it with anything abrasive. A gentle washing in a mild detergent bath is enough. After that I dry it briefly over a hot flame, then I rub about 1/2 teaspoon of oil into the surface with a paper towel.

But where I really prefer to cook my pancakes is on my old Farberware electric griddle, blackened from years of use. The advantage of electric is absolute and even heat control: I just set it at 375° F. and go. Size is the other big plus. I can make 6 pancakes at a time on my electric griddle; about the most I can manage in even the largest skillet is 3. At that rate, when I'm feeding a crowd, I have to fire up additional skillets to avoid a breakfast mutiny on my hands.

With a burner and skillet, the standard readiness test is to sprinkle a drop of water in the pan. A very active response, sizzling and bouncing, is supposed to signal a sufficiently hot surface. A rather lukewarm, fizzling response means it is not hot enough. This water test is only so reliable, because there's no clear indication when the pan is too hot. You can use the water test to get an idea of where you stand, but expect to do the fine tuning with your first pancake or two.

On the Griddle. Pancakes generally take about 1 1/2 to 2 1/2 minutes on side one, a little less on the second side. When little air holes start to show up on the surface and the very edge takes on a dryish tinge, they're ready to flip. Only flip them once and avoid any inclination to poke, prod, or press on them — that spells doom for pancakes. It only takes an initial light rub of oil on your cooking surface to keep them from sticking. After that, the fat in the batter prevents sticking.

On the Plate. Pancakes are precious little things, with little mass, so they begin to lose heat quickly once they're off the griddle. And a cold pancake, we all know, holds none of the promise and allure of a hot, steamy stack. Therefore, have warm plates waiting in the oven if at all possible (10 minutes in a 250° F. oven will do the trick). Also, have your pancake eaters assembled nearby, and whisk them to the table as soon as the stacks hit the plates. Finally, have *soft* butter on the table. I always hate it when I forget this and have to watch somebody hack up a perfect stack, spreading a cold, hard pat of butter on a delicate pancake. It makes me cringe.

A Word or Two About Syrup. If you want your syrup to go farther on pancakes and waffles, warm it up first, so it thins out. Warm syrup won't rob heat from your pancakes the way cold syrup will. You can either heat your syrup in a saucepan over low heat (don't let it come to a boil) and spoon it out, or keep a small amount in a table dispenser and warm that in a pan of hot water. I'm all in favor of those spring-loaded, glass dispensers you see in diners. Since the spring holds the top shut, there's no chance of accidentally spilling the valuable contents all over the table. This is especially useful if you have young kids. We have three, and our breakfast table is a regular reacharama. Stuff flies everywhere.

Some Waffle Thoughts. There are certain things I like more about waffles than pancakes, the main thing being they aren't so fussy. You can make up a batch of waffles and hold them in the oven on a wire rack for a reasonable amount of time — up to 15 minutes, say, at about 250° F. — without having them turn to rubber like pancakes will. Waffles even taste great at room temperature, or slightly warm; pancakes don't. Therefore, leftover waffles are never a problem. You can even pop them in the toaster the next day to warm them up, and they'll regain at least some of their crisp. They're not quite the same as fresh, but you could do much worse.

One thing about waffles: You'll need a waffle iron. Waffle irons come in all sorts of sizes and configurations, from heart shapes to squares and rectangles. They're available with the regular style grids, or in the deeper, larger Belgian waffle style. Some grids have a non-stick surface and need no special seasoning or oiling to keep the waffles from sticking, whereas the old-fashioned type, of bare cast iron or aluminum, is conditioned — according to the manufacturer's directions — to build a seasoned, stick-resistant surface that's never washed. With this type, the grids are usually brushed lightly with vegetable oil before heating.

My experience with waffle irons is limited (it's not the sort of thing most people keep more than one of around), but I can tell you I like the bigger irons with a nonstick surface. Originally, I thought such a surface might interfere with a waffle's ability to crispen, but this hasn't been the case.

All waffle irons have their own little quirks, which you'll learn when you buy one. But basically, you just preheat the thing and ladle on the batter, only using enough batter to fill the grid once the iron has been closed. Otherwise, when you lower the lid it all runs out the sides. If that happens, just let it cook on there and pull it off later. You'll quickly learn how much batter is needed to fill the grid.

One final caution: Be careful about yard sale waffle irons. Maybe I'm being paranoid, but I once bought one, only to find that the nonstick surface was anything but. It took days of soaking and scrubbing to get the cooked-on batter out of the grids. Imagine my state of utter despair, thinking that I was only minutes away from a towering plate of Death By Chocolate Waffles (page 127).

BASIC WHOLE WHEAT PANCAKES

Preparation time: 10 minutes
Cooking time: 3 to 4 minutes per batch   **Yield:** About 14 four-inch pancakes

These pancakes are like home to me. After I've been spinning off all sorts of pancake variations for a while, they're comforting to come back to. They have an honest, grainy flavor, just the right amount of crunch and a pleasant, cakey texture. Remember that whole grain flours vary widely in their absorptive capabilities, so the batter may have to be thinned with a little milk to reach the proper consistency.

1 cup cornmeal, preferably
   stone-ground
1½ cups whole wheat flour
½ teaspoon salt
1 tablespoon baking powder
3 large eggs
1¾ cups milk
2 tablespoons molasses
¼ cup oil or butter, melted

Stir together the cornmeal, whole wheat flour, salt, and baking powder. In a separate bowl, beat the eggs well and blend in the milk and molasses. Make a well in the dry ingredients, then pour in the liquids, including the oil or butter, and stir just until smooth. Let stand for several minutes before cooking on a hot griddle.

JEANNE'S OATMEAL PANCAKES

Preparation time: 10 minutes
Cooking time: 3 to 4 minutes per batch   **Yield:** 14 four-inch cakes

This great recipe comes from my friend Jeanne Lemlin, author of Vegetarian Pleasures *(Knopf, 1986), known far and wide for her inspired vegetarian cooking. She makes my kind of hotcakes, grainy and nicely textured. You'll want to make these often, once you've tried them.*

1 cup rolled oats (non-instant)
1 cup unbleached or all-
   purpose flour
½ cup whole wheat flour
2½ teaspoons baking
   powder
1 teaspoon salt
2 large eggs
2 cups milk
2 tablespoons brown sugar
5 tablespoons butter, melted

Whirl the oats in a blender until they become a fine powder; a few traces of flakes are fine. Pour into a large bowl; then mix in the flours, baking powder, and salt. Set aside.

In a medium-size bowl, beat the eggs lightly, then whisk in the milk and brown sugar. Make a well in the dry ingredients, pour in the liquids, and stir briefly. Add the melted butter and blend just until no traces of dry are visible. Let the batter sit for several minutes, then cook on a hot griddle.

SUSAN'S BANANA NUT PANCAKES

Preparation time: 10 minutes
Cooking time: About 5 minutes per batch   **Yield:** 12 to 14 four-inch pancakes

This recipe comes from Susan Cunningham, one of the owners of The Inn at Goodwin Park, a cozy inn located in Portsmouth, New Hampshire, operating in the traditional British B&B style. Known for their fine breakfasts, Susan and company might serve these tasty pancakes to their guests along with baked Frangelico-flavored pears or a medley of fresh, native berries.

1 cup unbleached or all-
  purpose flour
1 cup whole wheat flour
2½ teaspoons baking powder
½ teaspoon baking soda
½ teaspoon salt
½ cup chopped walnuts
  or pecans
2 large eggs
¼ cup maple syrup
4 tablespoons unsalted
  butter, melted
1⅓ to 1½ cups milk
¾ cup sour cream
1 ripe banana, mashed

Combine the dry ingredients in a mixing bowl and toss to mix. In a separate bowl, beat the eggs until frothy, then whisk in the remaining ingredients, using 1⅓ cups milk; the batter can be thinned, if needed, with the extra milk. Make a well in the dry mixture, then pour in the liquids. Stir, just to blend; do not beat. Let the batter sit for several minutes, then cook on a hot griddle.

BUCKWHEAT COCOA PANCAKES

Preparation time: 10 minutes
Cooking time: 3 to 4 minutes per batch   **Yield:** About 18 five-inch cakes

At the risk of stepping on some traditionalist toes, I must tell you I've long thought buckwheat pancakes were their own worst enemy. The problem is buckwheat. It has a strong, grassy flavor — too much so for an all-buckwheat pancake. So, I came up with this, a pancake where the buckwheat flavor comes across in a congenial kind of way, with the cocoa providing just the right accent.

½ cup buckwheat flour
½ cup whole wheat flour
½ cup unbleached or all-
  purpose flour
1 tablespoon unsweetened
  cocoa
2 teaspoons baking powder
½ teaspoon baking soda
½ teaspoon salt
2 large eggs
1¼ cups milk
1 cup buttermilk
2 tablespoons sugar
¼ cup vegetable oil

Combine the flours, cocoa, baking powder, baking soda, and salt in a large mixing bowl. Toss to mix. In a separate bowl, beat the eggs, then whisk in the remaining ingredients. Make a well in the dry mixture, then stir in the liquids with a few deft strokes. Let the batter sit for several minutes, then cook on a hot griddle.

RICOTTA BLENDER CAKES

Preparation time: 5 minutes
Cooking time: 3 to 5 minutes per batch   **Yield:** About 15 five-inch cakes

These creamy, rich-tasting pancakes can be made in a flash. Delicate in flavor, they have a natural affinity for fresh berries in season, dished up next to and on top of your stack. You can replace the ricotta with cottage cheese if you wish.

1½ cups ricotta cheese
4 large eggs
½ cup milk
2 tablespoons white or brown sugar
4 tablespoons unsalted butter, melted, or vegetable oil
½ teaspoon finely grated lemon zest (optional)
1 cup whole wheat flour
2 teaspoons baking powder
½ teaspoon salt

Combine the ricotta cheese, eggs, milk, sugar, butter or oil, and lemon zest in a blender and process until smooth. Mix the remaining ingredients in a large bowl, make a well in the center, then whisk in the liquids. Stir just until combined. Let the batter sit for several minutes, then cook on a hot griddle.

WHEATEN BUTTERMILK CORN CAKES

Preparation time: 10 minutes
Cooking time: 3 to 4 minutes per batch   **Yield:** About 18 four-inch cakes

Here is a lovely buttermilk pancake, one I've been making for many years. It differs from other corn cakes in that the cornmeal is precooked, giving the pancakes a soft and moist, instead of cakey, texture.

½ cup cornmeal, preferably
   stone-ground
1 cup cold water
¼ cup blackstrap molasses
⅔ cup buttermilk
⅔ cup milk
2 large eggs, lightly beaten
¼ cup unsalted butter,
   melted, or vegetable oil
1¼ cups whole wheat flour
1½ teaspoons baking powder
½ teaspoon baking soda
½ teaspoon salt

In a small, heavy saucepan, stir together the cornmeal and cold water. Bring to a boil, reduce the heat to medium, and cook, stirring constantly, for 2 to 3 minutes, until quite thick. Scrape into a large mixing bowl; then whisk in, individually, the molasses, buttermilk, milk, eggs, and butter or oil.

In a separate large bowl, combine the remaining ingredients and toss to mix. Make a well in this dry mixture, add the liquids, and stir just until blended. Let the batter sit for several minutes, then thin with a tablespoon or two of milk, if needed; the batter should run thickly off the ladle. Cook on a hot griddle.

A MEGABATCH OF PANCAKES

Preparation time: 15 minutes   **Cooking time:** About 5 minutes per batch   **Yield:** 75 pancakes

A special thanks to my friend Margaret Fox for providing this large-quantity recipe for cornmeal pancakes. Margaret is the chef/owner of the now-famous Café Beaujolais, in Mendocino, California, where her great breakfasts have been drawing large, hungry crowds for several years now. Of course, not everybody needs a recipe for 75 (or 150) pancakes, but now you know where to turn when your next community pancake event rolls around.

7½ cups unbleached or
   all-purpose flour
2 tablespoons baking powder
1 cup plus 2 tablespoons
   white sugar
1 tablespoon baking soda
1 tablespoon salt
6 cups cornmeal
18 eggs, separated
12 cups buttermilk
¾ cup butter, melted

Sift together all the dry ingredients and set aside. Mix together the egg yolks, buttermilk, and melted butter and add to the dry ingredients, stirring just until combined. Beat the egg whites until stiff (but not dry) and fold in gently. Cook on a hot griddle. Note: Margaret says this recipe can be doubled for twice the amount without any significant adjustments.

WHOLE WHEAT CORN WAFFLES

Preparation time: 10 minutes
Cooking time: 4 to 5 minutes per batch   **Yield:** 4 to 5 servings

These wholesome waffles have a wonderful crunch and a deep, grainy flavor. They're great with a little plain yogurt on the side.

1½ cups whole wheat flour
½ cup cornmeal, preferably stone-ground
2 tablespoons sugar
4 teaspoons baking powder
¾ teaspoon salt
2 large eggs
2⅓ cups milk
8 tablespoons unsalted butter, melted (or part butter and part vegetable oil)

Combine the flour, cornmeal, sugar, baking powder, and salt in a large mixing bowl and toss to mix. In a separate bowl, beat the eggs lightly. Whisk in the milk and butter. Make a well in the dry ingredients, then pour in the liquids. Whisk briefly, just until blended. Let the batter sit for several minutes, then cook on a hot waffle iron.

VERY CRISP OAT & CORN WAFFLES

Preparation time: 10 minutes
Cooking time: About 5 minutes per batch   **Yield:** 4 to 5 servings

Corn and oats are an unbeatable duo, as you'll discover when you make these. This version is somewhat rich, but you can replace the cream with milk if you like. The waffles' supercrispness makes them a natural partner for fresh berries, applesauce, Pan-Fried Apple Rings (see page 30), and yogurt.

1¼ cups rolled oats
   (non-instant)
½ cup cornmeal, preferably
   stone-ground
½ cup unbleached or all-
   purpose flour
4 teaspoons baking powder
3 tablespoons sugar
¾ teaspoon salt
2 large eggs, at room
   temperature
1 cup heavy cream
1 cup plus 2 tablespoons milk
6 tablespoons unsalted butter,
   melted

Whirl the oats in a blender until powdered; some remaining larger flakes are actually desirable. Toss with the cornmeal, flour, baking powder, sugar, and salt to combine.

In a separate bowl, beat the eggs with a whisk until frothy. Whisk in the cream, milk, and butter. Make a well in the dry mixture, add the liquids, and stir with a few strokes, just until smooth. Let the batter sit for several minutes, then cook on a hot waffle iron until well browned.

DEATH BY CHOCOLATE WAFFLES

Preparation time: 10 minutes
Cooking time: About 4 minutes per batch   **Yield:** 4 to 5 servings

Well, maybe not life threatening, but surely diet threatening! Try these crisp, double-chocolate waffles with a small mountain of vanilla ice cream and a pool of maple syrup. The ultimate in chocolate decadence.

1⅓ cups unbleached or
    all-purpose flour
⅓ cup whole wheat flour
¼ cup unsweetened cocoa
1 tablespoon baking powder
1 teaspoon cinnamon
½ teaspoon salt
8 tablespoons unsalted butter
3 ounces semisweet chocolate
2 tablespoons sugar
2¼ cups milk
2 large eggs, beaten until
    frothy

In a large mixing bowl, combine the flours, cocoa, baking powder, cinnamon, and salt. Toss to mix. Set aside.

Combine the butter, chocolate, and sugar in a heavy-bottomed saucepan and melt over very low heat. Whisk to smooth, remove from the heat, then whisk in the milk and eggs.

Make a well in the dry mixture, pour in the liquids and blend, just until everything is combined; watch for dry clumps. Let batter sit for several minutes; it will thicken slightly. Then cook on a hot waffle iron. Serve at once.

LACY SWEET POTATO BREAKFAST PATTIES

Preparation time: 10 minutes   **Cooking time:** 7 to 8 minutes per batch   **Yield:** 3 to 4 servings

These savory pancakes are designed to be served with just a drizzle of maple syrup, so they're a good choice when you're not in the mood for an overly sweet breakfast. They go well with almost any egg dish, a side of applesauce, breakfast meats, toast, and biscuits. The pancake mixture isn't terribly cohesive, but as long as you don't manhandle the patties, or make them overly huge, they'll hold together just fine.

1 large sweet potato
   (about ½ pound)
¼ teaspoon salt
1 large egg
2 tablespoons heavy or
   light cream
1 tablespoon cornmeal
½ cup minced ham or
   Canadian bacon
1 tablespoon minced onion
Salt and pepper
Oil and butter for frying

Wash the sweet potato and remove any bad spots, then grate it into a bowl. Mix in the salt and set aside for 5 minutes. While that sits, beat the egg lightly, then whisk in the cream and cornmeal. Using your hands, squeeze the moisture out of the grated potato, then add to the egg mixture. Stir in the ham, onion, and a pinch of salt and pepper.

Heat about a tablespoon of oil in a heavy skillet over medium heat. Add a tablespoon of butter, let it melt, then — using about ¼ cup of the patty mixture per pancake — spoon the mixture into the skillet; don't crowd the pancakes. Spread and flatten the patties with a fork to the thickness of about ¼ inch. They should be no wider than your spatula. Fry for 3 to 4 minutes per side, flipping only once; they'll be dark and crusty on the outside. Serve hot. The patties hold up for a little while in a hot oven, if you want to serve them all at once.

APPLEJACK-SPIKED BAKED APPLES

Preparation time: 20 minutes   **Baking time:** About 50 minutes   **Yield:** 4 servings

Most baked apples I can take or leave, but this one — lavishly bathed in a heady combination of applejack, maple, butter, and vanilla — is in a class by itself. One of the important steps here is to cool the apples before you serve them, and continue to baste with the thickening juices. Excellent with a dollop of cold sour cream or lightly sweetened whipped cream.

¼ cup finely chopped walnuts
   or pecans
¼ cup finely chopped dates
3 tablespoons unsalted butter
4 large baking apples
⅓ cup maple syrup
¼ cup water
⅓ cup applejack
1 teaspoon vanilla extract
¼ teaspoon cinnamon

Preheat the oven to 375° F. Combine the walnuts or pecans and dates in a small bowl. Rub about ½ tablespoon of the butter into the date-nut mixture, so it all pulls together. Set aside.

Core the apples, a little on the wide side, then peel the upper third of each one; this will help prevent them from bursting. Cut the very bottom 1/16th inch off the bottom of each apple, so they sit flat in the pan. Divide the reserved date-nut mixture among the 4 cavities, stuffing it down into each one; hold one hand at the bottom, so it doesn't push out. The filling should come a little below the top of the apple, so there's a little space left to hold the basting juice. Place the apples in a large pie dish.

Bring the maple syrup, water, and remaining 2½ tablespoons butter to a boil in a saucepan. Boil briefly, remove from the heat, then stir in the applejack, vanilla, and cinnamon. Pour this over the apples, baste, then put the pan in the oven. Bake for about 50 minutes, basting every 10 minutes or so. Remove from the oven and cool, periodically basting with the juices as they thicken. Serve lukewarm, at room temperature, or — my favorite way — cold, for breakfast. Spoon any leftover juice over them when served.

PAN-FRIED APPLE RINGS

Preparation time: 15 minutes   **Yield:** 2 to 3 servings

Here are three different versions of apple rings: one plain, one saucy, and one crunchy. All wonderful. They're sweet enough that, for breakfast, you wouldn't want to serve them on the side with anything else sweet. They're best with breakfast meats, eggs, or yogurt.

1 large, firm cooking apple, cored
½ cup water
⅓ cup maple syrup
2 tablespoons butter

Trim a little off the ends of the apple, then cut the apple into slices a scant ½ inch thick; you'll have 5 or 6. Set aside.

Heat the water, maple syrup, and butter in a heavy, 9-inch or 10-inch skillet. Stir to blend, bringing it to a boil. When it reaches a boil, add the apple rings, in one layer. Reduce the heat to a low-moderate boil and cook, uncovered, until the liquid is reduced to a thick syrup, turning the rings several times to glaze them. Watch that the apples don't get mushy or the syrup burns. Transfer to a serving plate, scraping the remaining glaze over them. Serve hot or warm.

Apple Rings with Maple Cream Sauce
Prepare and cook as above. Before the syrup starts to coat the pan very thickly, transfer the rings to a warm plate, then pour ½ cup of light cream into the pan. Bring to a boil and cook, stirring constantly, for 15 seconds. Reduce the heat to an active simmer and cook, stirring, for a minute or two longer. The finished sauce will have the consistency of heavy cream. Be careful to avoid burning. Spoon the hot sauce over the rings and serve right away.

Apple Rings with Graham Cracker Crumb Topping
This could almost be considered a dessert, or a one-dish breakfast. Think of apple crisp, with lots of graham crackers in the topping — that's what this is like.

Before you begin, gently heat 2 tablespoons butter with 1 tablespoon maple syrup in a small saucepan just until the butter melts. Stir in ¾ cup fine graham cracker crumbs and continue stirring until the mixture is smooth. Remove from the heat and set aside.

Preheat the broiler. Cook the apple rings as above. When heavily glazed, remove from the heat and spread the reserved crumbs evenly over the apples. Broil briefly, just until crumbs darken a shade or two. Watch carefully so it doesn't burn. Serve hot or warm.

OVEN SKILLET APPLE PANCAKE

Preparation time: 15 minutes   **Baking time:** 15 to 18 minutes   **Yield:** 4 to 6 servings

I've always loved the rustic look of this pancake as much as I have the flavor. It's one of the prettier things you'll ever aim a jug of syrup at. Simple to make, too, for a fast breakfast or even a last minute dessert. It puffs up beautifully in the oven, but doesn't stay that way for long. You can serve this sliced, right from the skillet, or invert it onto a plate (first loosen underneath with a spatula).

2 firm cooking apples, peeled, cored, and sliced
2 tablespoons maple syrup
1 tablespoon lemon juice
4 tablespoons unsalted butter
3 large eggs
½ cup milk or light cream
½ cup unbleached or all-purpose flour
½ teaspoon cinnamon
¼ teaspoon salt

Preheat the oven to 425° F. Toss the apples with the maple syrup and lemon juice and set aside. Melt the butter in a 9-inch or 10-inch cast-iron skillet and remove from the heat.

Beat the eggs and milk in a bowl with 1 tablespoon of the melted butter. In a separate bowl, combine the flour, cinnamon, and salt and whisk in the egg mixture until smooth.

Return the skillet to the heat and sauté the apples in the butter over high heat. After 2 or 3 minutes, before they get mushy, spread the apples evenly in the pan and slowly pour on the batter. Bake for 15 to 18 minutes, until very puffy and lightly browned. Serve hot or warm directly from the pan, drizzled with maple syrup.

CINNAMON-FRIED CORNMEAL MUSH

Preparation time: 25 minutes, plus overnight chilling
Frying time: 6 to 8 minutes per batch   **Yield:** 8 servings

I love corny things, and these luscious slices — dredged in cinnamon-spiked cornmeal, delicately fried in butter, then doused with maple syrup — are high up on my list of breakfast favorites. They're perfect with breakfast meats and eggs, or with applesauce, berries, or yogurt on the side. A few other things to know: You must start this the night before. This will last in the refrigerator for several days, so you can slice and fry anytime. And be sure to use fresh, stone-ground cornmeal, available in health food stores.

4 cups water
1 teaspoon salt
2 cups coarsely ground
   cornmeal
About 3 tablespoons unsalted
   butter
1½ teaspoons cinnamon
Maple syrup for drizzling
   on top

Butter a large, shallow casserole, measuring either 8 inches by 12 inches or 9 inches by 13 inches. Heat the water in a large, heavy-bottomed pot. Add the salt. As the water heats, sprinkle in 1½ cups of the cornmeal, a little at a time, whisking all the while.

When the mixture reaches a boil, switch to a wooden spoon. Reduce the heat down to medium-low and cook the mush, stirring continuously, for 15 minutes; the mixture will become quite thick. Stir in 1 tablespoon of the butter until melted, then remove from the heat. Immediately scrape the mush into the prepared casserole and flatten the top as best you can with a spatula. Cool to room temperature, cover, and refrigerate overnight.

The next morning, stir the cinnamon into the remaining ½ cup cornmeal. Cut the chilled cornmeal mush into serving-size pieces — roughly 2 inches by 3 inches is a good size, but anywhere around there is fine. Melt about 2 tablespoons of butter in a cast-iron skillet over medium-low heat. Dredge the slices in the cinnamon mix, then fry them in the butter, without crowding, 3 to 4 minutes on each side. Serve hot, drizzled with maple syrup.

OAT MAPLE-WALNUT MUFFINS

Preparation time: 15 minutes   **Baking time:** 20 minutes   **Yield:** 12 muffins

I love oats in breads. The subtle oat flavor really shines here, reinforced beautifully by a sweet maple note. Very fragrant, these will draw a crowd to your kitchen at any hour.

1¼ cups rolled oats
  (non-instant)
1 cup whole wheat flour
½ cup unbleached or all-
  purpose flour
1 teaspoon baking soda
1 teaspoon baking powder
1 teaspoon salt
2 large eggs
1 cup buttermilk
½ cup maple syrup
¼ cup vegetable oil
½ cup finely chopped walnuts

Preheat the oven to 400° F. Butter 12 muffin cups and set aside. Process the rolled oats in a blender until the oats are reduced to a rough powder; it is fine if some larger flakes remain. Measure out exactly 1 cup of this oat flour and put it in a large mixing bowl with the other flours, baking soda, baking powder, and salt. Toss to mix.

Beat the eggs in a separate bowl, then blend in the buttermilk, maple syrup, and oil. Make a well in the dry ingredients, pour in the liquids, and stir just to blend. Fold in the walnuts. Divide the batter evenly among the muffin cups. Bake for 20 minutes, until golden. Serve hot.

QUICK BISCUIT STICKY BUNS

Preparation time: 25 to 30 minutes   **Baking time:** 25 minutes   **Yield:** 9 servings

If you like sticky buns but can seldom find the time to make the real thing, these are for you. We take an ordinary biscuit recipe and turn it into something quite extraordinary with the help of a maple-butter glaze. And we seal the deal with a brown sugar, walnut, and cinnamon filling. You'll want to make these for a special Sunday breakfast.

½ cup finely chopped walnuts
¼ cup brown sugar
½ teaspoon cinnamon
½ cup maple syrup
9 tablespoons cold unsalted butter
2¼ cups unbleached or all-purpose flour
1 tablespoon baking powder
¾ teaspoon salt
1 cup milk

Mix together the walnuts, brown sugar, and cinnamon in a small bowl. Set aside. Preheat the oven to 400° F.

In a small saucepan, bring the maple syrup and 4 tablespoons of the butter to a boil over medium heat. Boil for 30 seconds, then scrape into a 9-inch by 9-inch baking pan or a 10-inch deep dish pie pan. Set aside.

Combine the flour, baking powder, and salt in a large mixing bowl and toss to mix. Cut 4 tablespoons of the butter into ½-inch pieces, add to the flour, and cut it in until the butter is roughly the size of split peas. Make a well in the mixture and add the milk. Stir gently, just until the mixture forms a damp, cohesive mass. If the dough seems a bit wet, work in a tad more flour with the back of a wooden spoon. Melt the remaining 1 tablespoon of butter in a small saucepan.

Turn the dough out onto a lightly floured surface and knead gently, 5 or 6 times. Using a rolling pin, roll out the dough to the best 9-inch by 12-inch rectangle you can manage; don't worry if it isn't perfect. Brush the surface with the melted butter. Cover the dough evenly with the brown sugar mixture, patting it gently with your hands. Starting at the 9-inch edge, roll the dough up like a carpet, pinching at the seam to seal. Cut into 9 one-inch-wide slices and lay them, on the flat, in the syruped pan. Bake for 25 minutes. Remove from the oven and invert onto a large plate; do this quickly, but carefully, being aware that the syrup is very hot. Rubber gloves are a good precaution. Scrape any syrupy stuff from the pan and spread over the buns. Serve hot or warm.

MAPLE CREAM BISCUITS

Preparation time: 10 minutes   **Baking time:** 15 minutes   **Yield:** About 12 biscuits

These soft, delicate biscuits are one of the most delicious ways I know to run up your cholesterol count. You can imagine how good they are, since they call for both cream and butter. Served with coffee they make a simple, satisfying breakfast.

2 cups all-purpose or
    unbleached flour
1 tablespoon baking powder
¾ teaspoon salt
4 tablespoons cold unsalted
    butter, cut into ¼-inch
    pieces
¾ cup heavy cream
¼ cup maple syrup
2 tablespoons unsalted butter,
    melted with 2 tablespoons
    maple syrup

Preheat the oven to 425° F. Combine the flour, baking powder, and salt in a large mixing bowl. Cut the butter into the flour until the mixture resembles a coarse meal. Make a well in this mixture.

Blend the heavy cream and ¼ cup maple syrup and pour them into the well. Stir, just until the dough coheres. Turn the dough out onto a lightly floured surface and knead 4 or 5 times, gently. Pat or roll to a thickness of about ¾ inch. Cut into 2½-inch to 3-inch rounds with a biscuit cutter and place on a lightly greased baking sheet. Stir the melted butter/maple syrup mixture to blend it, then brush a little on each biscuit. Bake for about 15 minutes, until golden. Serve hot. Pass the remaining warm butter and syrup, to spoon over the split biscuits.

CANADIAN BACON CHEESE DREAM

Preparation time: 10 minutes   **Cooking time:** About 5 minutes   **Yield:** 2 servings

Reading through some old James Beard columns, I came across a reference to a once popular sandwich he called a cheese dream — a combination of cheddar cheese, sliced tomato, and bacon. Inspired by that thought, I spun off this breakfast version, and let me tell you, our friends with the golden arches have nothing on this. If your tomatoes aren't that great — which tends to be the case for about 49 out of 52 weeks a year — they might benefit from a quick flash in the pan with the bacon.

1½ tablespoons maple syrup
1 tablespoon water
2 teaspoons lemon juice or cider vinegar
1½ teaspoons Dijon-style mustard
Pinch ground cloves
Pinch cayenne
1 tablespoon butter
2 thick slices Canadian bacon
1 English muffin, halved and toasted
2 eggs fried, over hard
2 thick slices tomato
1 cup grated cheddar cheese, preferably smoked

In a small bowl, whisk together the maple syrup, water, lemon juice or cider vinegar, mustard, and spices. Set aside.

Melt the butter in a heavy skillet over medium heat and add the bacon. Fry gently, about 1 minute per side, then pour in the sauce. Increase the heat and continue to cook until the liquid reduces to a thick glaze. Remove from the heat.

Preheat the broiler. Place the toasted muffin halves in a pie plate. Swish the bacon slices in the glaze, then lay a slice on each muffin half. Top each with a fried egg and a slice of tomato, then spread the cheese over the top. Broil just until the cheese melts. Serve at once.

GOLDEN CORNMEAL CAKE

Preparation time: 20 minutes   **Baking time:** 50 to 60 minutes   **Yield:** 12 or more servings

Here's a special occasion breakfast cake worth rolling out of bed for. Sometimes I decrease the amount of coconut and replace it with chopped walnuts.

1 cup unsalted butter, at room temperature
1 cup maple syrup, at room temperature
3 large eggs, at room temperature
2 teaspoons vanilla extract
Finely grated zest of 1 orange
1¼ cups unbleached or all-purpose flour
¾ cup cornmeal, preferably stone-ground
1 tablespoon baking powder
½ teaspoon salt
1½ cups shredded sweetened coconut (available in health food stores)
¾ cup sour cream
1 cup raisins

Preheat the oven to 350° F. Butter a large tube pan or a 10-inch bundt pan and set aside.

Cream the butter with an electric mixer, gradually adding the maple syrup. Beat in the eggs, one at a time, then the vanilla and orange zest.

In a separate bowl, sift together the flour, cornmeal, baking powder, and salt. Toss in the coconut. Add the dry ingredients to the creamed mixture alternately with the sour cream, in 2 or 3 stages, each time just stirring to blend. Don't beat it. Fold in the raisins. Bake for 50 to 60 minutes, until a tester comes out clean. Cool briefly in the pan, then turn out onto a plate and serve.

A GALLON OF GRANOLA

Preparation time: 15 minutes   **Baking time:** 30 to 40 minutes   **Yield:** 1 gallon

Every Christmas I like to prepare large batches of this for my friends and family; it makes a great stocking stuffer. Instead of all oats you can also use other grain flakes. Some of the seeds can be replaced by bran or untoasted wheat germ.

8 cups rolled oats
  (non-instant)
2 cups coarsely chopped nuts
  (cashews, pecans, or
  almonds)
2 cups raw (untoasted)
  sunflower seeds
1 cup sesame seeds
1 cup shredded unsweetened
  coconut (available in health
  food stores)
1 teaspoon salt
¾ cup maple syrup
¾ cup light-tasting vegetable
  oil, such as sunflower oil
2 cups chopped dried fruit
  (raisins, currants, and dates
  are good)

Preheat the oven to 300° F. In a large mixing bowl, toss together the oats, nuts, sunflower seeds, sesame seeds, coconut, and salt. Warm the maple syrup and oil together in a saucepan. Pour over the dry ingredients. Stir with a wooden spoon, then roll up your sleeves and work the mixture with your hands until everything is damp. Spread on baking sheets — no more than about ½ inch thick — and roast for 30 to 40 minutes, stirring occasionally, until golden. When the granola has cooled, stir in the dried fruit. Store in jars or plastic bags.

Cookies

Reach your hand into a jarful —
from Whole Wheat Maple Snickerdoodles
to Cindy's Coffee Chip Cookies

MAPLE MYSTERY BITES

Preparation time: 20 minutes   **Baking time:** 55 to 60 minutes total   **Yield:** 16 bars

This recipe is adapted from one given me by Ed Brown, the Zen monk who wrote all those wonderful Tassajara cookbooks. His original version called for a lot more spice and honey. It was great. So is this "maplized" version: a short crust under a gooey walnut and date topping. I've also substituted pecans and nobody has complained.

1 cup unbleached or all-
    purpose flour
¼ cup brown sugar
Pinch salt
8 tablespoons cold unsalted
    butter
2 large eggs
¾ cup maple syrup
1 teaspoon vanilla extract
3 tablespoons unbleached or
    all-purpose flour
1 teaspoon baking powder
½ cup chopped walnuts
½ cup chopped dates

Preheat the oven to 325° F. Combine the 1 cup flour, brown sugar, and salt in a mixing bowl. Rub with your fingers to mix. Cut the cold butter into the dry mixture until it is somewhat sandy in texture and begins clumping together. Transfer to an ungreased 8-inch by 8-inch baking pan, distribute evenly, then press into the bottom of the pan with your fingers. Bake in the middle of the oven for 25 to 30 minutes, until shaded with the edges starting to brown. Cool on a rack to room temperature.

Beat the eggs until frothy in a large mixing bowl. Whisk in the maple syrup and vanilla. Combine the 3 tablespoons flour and baking powder in a sieve and shake it over the maple mix, whisking it in. Fold in the walnuts and dates. Pour over the crust, distribute evenly, and bake for 30 minutes, until a tester comes out clean. Cool on a rack, then cut into sixteen 2-inch squares.

ALMOND NIRVANA

Preparation time: 35 minutes, plus cooling time
Baking time: About 35 minutes total   **Yield:** 2 to 3 dozen bars

Warning: You could easily put on several pounds just reading this recipe, let alone eating it. They're entirely out of the question if you value your waistline. On the other hand, this is a large recipe, to be cut in small pieces, so you could stash away a piece or two for yourself and put out the rest for a Christmas or New Year's gathering. I specify a 10-inch by 15-inch jelly roll pan, but I have actually used an 11-inch by 17-inch pan. It's not a difficult recipe, but you should read the instructions through before starting, just to get the hang of the technique.

Crust
1 cup unsalted butter, at room
    temperature
½ cup brown sugar, packed
1 large egg, at room
    temperature
3 cups unbleached or all-
    purpose flour

Topping
½ cup unsalted butter
¾ cup maple syrup
½ cup brown sugar
¼ cup honey
¼ cup heavy cream
2 cups chopped almonds
1 teaspoon vanilla extract

Lightly butter a 10-inch by 15-inch jelly roll pan. Preheat the oven to 375° F.

Cream the 1 cup butter and ½ cup brown sugar together. When light, beat in the egg. Add the flour, about ½ cup at a time, working it in with a wooden spoon. Divide the dough in 4 pieces and put a piece in each quadrant of the jelly roll pan. Now push the dough into the pan with floured hands, forming a seamless crust. Keep it as even as you can and work it up the sides to the top of the rim. It won't look perfect, but just do the best job you can; if you want to flatten it out some, roll it with a pin. Cover with plastic and chill for 15 minutes. Poke the dough 3 or 4 times with a fork, then bake for 15 minutes. Cool on a rack. Mix a tiny amount of flour and water together to make a thick paste, and rub a little into the fork holes to close them up.

After the crust has cooled for 20 or so minutes, melt the remaining ½ cup butter in a large saucepan. Add the maple syrup, ½ cup brown sugar, and honey and bring to a boil. When it boils, add the cream and bring back to a boil. Boil for 2 minutes. Quickly remove from heat and stir in the almonds and vanilla. Spread evenly over the crust and bake for 20 minutes; it will bubble and darken somewhat. Cool thoroughly on a rack, then cut into bars.

GORP BARS

Preparation time: 10 minutes   **Baking time:** 30 minutes   **Yield:** About 2 dozen bars

Good Old Raisins and Peanuts bars. Moist and chewy, they are great for brown baggers.

1 cup unsalted, unsweetened peanut butter (smooth or crunchy)
½ cup unsalted butter, at room temperature
1 cup maple syrup
1 large egg
1 teaspoon vanilla extract
½ teaspoon baking soda
1 cup rolled oats (non-instant)
1 cup whole wheat or unbleached flour
1½ cups finely chopped, raw unsalted peanuts
1½ cups raisins

Preheat the oven to 350° F. Butter a 9-inch by 13-inch baking pan and set it aside.

Cream the peanut butter and butter with an electric mixer. Gradually add the maple syrup, egg, vanilla, and baking soda. Stir in the oats and flour, just to blend, followed by the peanuts and raisins. Using floured hands, pat the mixture evenly into the prepared pan. Bake for about 30 minutes, just until the edges begin to brown. Cool on a rack before cutting into bars.

PECAN PIE SHORTBREAD

Preparation time: 20 minutes
Baking time: About 40 minutes   **Yield:** 1½ to 2 dozen small bars

This is neat: a shortbread on the bottom, a thin pecan pie layer on top. Quite rich, they're best cut in small squares. Nice for nibblers around the holidays.

1 cup unsalted butter, at room temperature
1 cup maple syrup, at room temperature
½ teaspoon salt
3 cups plus 1 tablespoon unbleached or all-purpose flour
1 large egg
1 teaspoon vanilla extract
4 tablespoons unsalted butter, melted
1½ cups chopped pecans

Preheat the oven to 350° F. Cream the 1 cup soft butter with an electric mixer. When somewhat fluffy, gradually drizzle in ½ cup of the maple syrup. Add the salt, and then 3 cups of flour, ½ cup at a time. If the mixture starts to clump up too much in the beaters, switch to a wooden spoon. With floured hands, pat the soft dough evenly into a lightly greased 8-inch by 12-inch baking pan. Refrigerate while you make the topping.

Again using an electric mixer, beat the egg for a minute. Continue to beat, adding the remaining ½ cup maple syrup, the vanilla, melted butter, and the remaining tablespoon of flour. Stir in the nuts. Spread evenly over the shortbread and bake for about 40 minutes, until the top is set. Cool on a rack before cutting into bars.

BEN'S BLACK BOTTOM CHEESECAKE BARS

Preparation time: 15 minutes   **Baking time:** 45 minutes   **Yield:** About 2 dozen bars

I don't mix chocolate with maple syrup too often, because chocolate tends to overpower the subtle taste of maple. When I do, though — such as in these scrumptious cheesecake bars — I really like to go all out. Anyway, I find that since the chocolate ends up underneath, you can still appreciate the maple-flavored cheese layer. These are excellent.

1 recipe Rich Maple Short Crust (page 56)
1 pound cream cheese, at room temperature
½ cup sour cream, at room temperature
2 large eggs, at room temperature
¾ cup maple syrup, at room temperature
1 teaspoon vanilla extract
1 teaspoon lemon juice
1½ to 2 cups semisweet chocolate chips

Prepare the short crust as directed and spread in a 9-inch by 13-inch pan. Preheat the oven to 425° F.

Using an electric mixer, beat the cream cheese until fairly light-textured. Beat in the sour cream and then the eggs, one at a time. Gradually beat in the maple syrup, followed by the vanilla and lemon juice.

Sprinkle the chocolate chips evenly over the crust. Slowly pour on the cheese mixture. Bake for 15 minutes, then reduce the heat to 350° and bake for 30 more minutes. The cake will be puffed and probably have developed cracks on the top. Cool on a rack, cover, then chill before cutting into bars.

KILLER BARS

Preparation time: 15 minutes   **Baking time:** About 30 to 35 minutes   **Yield:** 2 dozen bars

Take a rich, buttery crust, add the lush gooeyness of a pecan pie, then throw in some nuts and chocolate for good measure and what do you have? Well, besides a potential weight problem, you have Killer Bars, a favorite holiday munchie around our place. These are the perfect goody to make for some sweet lover on your Christmas shopping list, if for no other reason than they are so decadent hardly anybody would make these for themself.

1 recipe Rich Maple Short
  Crust (page 56)
2 large eggs
1 cup maple syrup
1 teaspoon vanilla extract
¼ cup unbleached or all-
  purpose flour
½ teaspoon baking powder
1 cup chopped unsalted nuts
  (but not peanuts — too
  pedestrian for this)
1 cup chopped dates
1 cup semisweet chocolate
  chips
½ cup shredded unsweetened
  coconut (available in health
  food stores)

Prepare the crust according to the directions. Have the crust well chilled, but remove it from the refrigerator at least 5 minutes before you plan to put it in the oven. Preheat the oven to 425° F.

Whisk together the eggs, maple syrup, and vanilla. Combine the flour and baking powder, and sprinkle into the egg mixture as you whisk. Fold in the remaining ingredients. Pour the topping over the crust and spread evenly. Bake for 15 minutes, then reduce the heat to 350° and bake for another 15 to 20 minutes, until set; the top will be golden. Cool thoroughly on a rack before cutting into bars.

CINDY'S COFFEE CHIP COOKIES

Preparation time: 15 minutes, plus time for dough to sit
Baking time: 15 minutes per batch   **Yield:** About 2½ dozen

This is a classic chocolate chip cookie recipe from my original maple book. It incorporates almost all of my gustatory weaknesses — butter, maple, coffee, chocolate, and walnuts — and, I suspect, accounts for no small share of my dentist's annual income. Dedicated to my friend Cindy, who'll take her coffee any way she can.

1 cup unsalted butter, at room temperature
1 cup maple syrup, at room temperature
1½ tablespoons powdered instant coffee
2 tablespoons hot water
2 teaspoons vanilla or almond extract
1½ cups whole wheat flour
1 cup unbleached or all-purpose flour
2 cups finely chopped walnuts
1 teaspoon baking soda
½ teaspoon salt
1½ cups semisweet chocolate chips

Preheat the oven to 350° F. Cream the butter with an electric mixer, slowly drizzling in the maple syrup. Dissolve the instant coffee in the hot water and beat that in, along with the vanilla or almond extract.

In a separate bowl, toss together the flours, walnuts, baking soda, and salt. Stir into the creamed mixture, in several stages, until the flour is incorporated. Stir in the chocolate chips; don't beat the batter. Let the batter sit for several minutes, then drop slightly mounded tablespoons of batter onto a greased baking sheet, leaving about 2 inches between the mounds. Bake for about 15 minutes — only one sheet at a time — just until the edges begin to brown. Transfer to a rack and cool.

WHOLE WHEAT MAPLE SNICKERDOODLES

Preparation time: 15 to 20 minutes, plus 30 minutes chilling time
Baking time: 10 minutes per batch   **Yield:** 3 dozen

Credit for this healthy recipe goes to my wife, Karen, whose greatest mission in life — I love to tease her — is to bring whole wheat awareness to the world. We have a running debate over how much whole wheat flour is appropriate for any given recipe; she always wants more than I do. No complaints here, however, for this tasty, attractive, and wholesome version of a childhood favorite.

2⅔ cups sifted whole wheat flour
1 teaspoon cream of tartar
1 teaspoon baking soda
½ teaspoon salt
½ teaspoon cinnamon
1 cup unsalted butter, at room temperature
⅔ cup maple syrup, at room temperature
2 large eggs, at room temperature
2 tablespoons sugar

Sift the whole wheat flour a second time with the cream of tartar, baking soda, salt, and cinnamon. Set aside.

In a medium-size mixing bowl, cream the butter until fluffy, scraping down the sides of the bowl. With the mixer still running, add the maple syrup in a thin stream, followed by the eggs, one at a time. Gradually stir the dry ingredients into the creamed mixture, stirring just until blended. Cover and refrigerate for 30 minutes.

Preheat the oven to 400° F. and put the sugar in a small bowl. With lightly floured hands, roll the dough into balls about 1¼ inches in diameter. Roll the balls in the sugar, then place on an ungreased baking sheet, leaving 2 inches between them. Bake for 10 minutes, just until the tops no longer yield to light finger pressure. Transfer to a rack and cool. Store in an airtight container.

SOFT ALMOND COOKIES

Preparation time: 20 minutes   **Baking time:** About 15 minutes per batch   **Yield:** About 3 dozen

As far as almond cookies go, this one is hard to beat. The cream cheese and lemon give it a tangy lift, and the texture is a pleasant combination of soft and crumbly. You can spiff these up some by pressing an almond in the middle of each cookie before you bake it. If you don't have a food processor to grind the nuts, a blender is fine, but it helps to add a little flour to each batch you buzz to prevent the nuts from clumping together.

½ cup unsalted butter, at room temperature
3 ounces cream cheese, at room temperature
¾ cup maple syrup, at room temperature
1 egg
1 teaspoon almond extract
2 teaspoons finely grated lemon zest
2 cups almond meal (finely ground almonds)
1½ cups unbleached or all-purpose flour
½ teaspoon salt
1 teaspoon baking powder

Preheat the oven to 350° F. Using an electric mixer, cream the butter and cream cheese. Continue to beat, adding the maple syrup in a slow drizzle. Next, beat in the egg, almond extract, and lemon zest.

Toss together the remaining ingredients, then add them to the creamed mixture, stirring just until everything is blended. Spoon tablespoonsful of dough onto a lightly greased baking sheet, leaving just a little room between them. Bake, only one sheet at a time, for about 15 minutes, until the bottoms are golden and the tops just slightly resistant to finger pressure. Transfer the baked cookies to a rack to cool.

WHEATEN OAT CHEWS

Preparation time: 15 minutes   **Baking time:** 13 to 15 minutes per batch   **Yield:** 2 dozen

While I am fond of telling people I invented this recipe for its healthy character, that's really only half the truth. The larger half is I actually set out to develop a cookie that I could successfully use for making ice cream sandwiches, which I adore. The cookies needed to be flat, sturdy, chewy, and delicious. These fit the bill. I can't tell you how good they are. Ice cream sandwich construction advice follows.

8 tablespoons unsalted
    butter, at room temperature
½ cup maple syrup, at room
    temperature
¼ cup sugar
1 cup rolled oats (non-instant)
¾ cup whole wheat flour
½ teaspoon salt
½ teaspoon baking soda
¼ teaspoon cinnamon
¾ cup semisweet chocolate
    chips (optional)

Preheat the oven to 350° F. Using an electric mixer, cream the butter, maple syrup, and sugar until light. In a separate bowl, mix the oats, whole wheat flour, salt, baking soda, and cinnamon. With a wooden spoon, work the dry ingredients into the creamed mixture, adding the chocolate chips, if desired. Mix until evenly blended.

Lightly butter a large baking sheet. Spoon slightly rounded tablespoons of batter onto the sheet, leaving about 4 inches between them; they'll spread quite a bit. Bake for 13 to 15 minutes, until the cookies have darkened by a shade or two of brown and the edges even more so. The centers may seem underbaked, but that's fine; they'll firm up.

Cool the cookies on the sheet for 5 minutes. Transfer to a rack. Cool thoroughly, then store in an airtight container.

Ice Cream Sandwiches

Divide the batter into 12 more or less equal-size balls, putting only about 4 at a time on the buttered baking sheet; these *really* spread. Flatten them a little and bake as directed. They may need a minute or so extra. Cool.

Now, go buy yourself a pint or two of your favorite super premium ice cream in round containers. While it is still frozen hard, saw off slabs right through the container, using a sharp serrated knife. About ¾ inch is a reasonable slab thickness, though mine have been known to exceed 2 inches. Peel off the paper, sandwich the ice cream between 2 cookies, and have a blast!

RICH MAPLE SHORT CRUST

Preparation time: 10 minutes   **Baking time:** Varies with recipe   **Yield:** 9-inch by 13-inch crust

Here is a good, maple-laced cookie bar crust that's a cinch to prepare. I use it, among other things, for Killer Bars (page 46) and Ben's Black Bottom Cheesecake Bars (page 45).

¾ cup unsalted butter, at room temperature
⅓ cup maple syrup, at room temperature
½ teaspoon vanilla extract
2 cups unbleached or all-purpose flour
½ teaspoon salt

Cream the butter with an electric mixer. Continue to beat, gradually adding the maple syrup and vanilla. Combine the flour and salt, then gradually add to the creamed mixture, working it in with a wooden spoon. Using floured hands, pat evenly into a 9-inch by 13-inch baking pan; roll with a can or bottle to even it out. Cover, then refrigerate until needed.

BART'S & DAR'S NONDAIRY MAPLE COOKIES

Preparation time: 10 minutes   **Baking time:** 12 to 15 minutes per batch   **Yield:** About 2 dozen

This recipe, invented by my friends, Bart and Dar, is solid evidence that people with dietary restrictions don't have to roll over and play dead. For me — whose baking generally rings like an ad from the National Dairy Council — it was a real shocker to learn that a cookie without butter, eggs, milk products, or salt could taste so full and rich. Being pared down to the basics, this cookie has the advantage of a clean maple flavor.

1¼ cups whole wheat flour
1¼ cups shredded
   unsweetened coconut
1 tablespoon baking powder
¾ cup maple syrup
¼ cup water
¼ cup vegetable oil

Preheat the oven to 350° F. Combine the whole wheat flour, coconut, and baking powder in a large mixing bowl and toss to mix.

In a separate bowl, whisk together the remaining ingredients, then stir them into the dry mixture, just until combined. Spoon rounded tablespoons of dough onto a greased baking sheet, leaving about 2 inches between them. Bake — only one sheet at a time — for 12 to 15 minutes, until slightly resistant to gentle finger pressure. Transfer to a rack and cool.

MAPLE PUMPKIN COOKIES

Preparation time: 15 minutes   **Baking time:** 15 to 20 minutes per batch   **Yield:** About 3 dozen

Here's a soft, rather unusual cookie, packed with autumn highlights and a whisper of spice. The cookies have a light, cakey texture, so you can easily pack away 5 or 6 at a sitting. Great with cider or a cold glass of milk, and a nice treat for the wood-cutting or leaf-raking crew.

1 cup maple syrup
1 cup pumpkin puree, canned
    or freshly cooked and cooled
1 egg
1 teaspoon vanilla extract
½ cup unsalted butter, at
    room temperature
1 cup whole wheat flour
1 cup unbleached or all-
    purpose flour
1 teaspoon baking soda
1 teaspoon baking powder
½ teaspoon salt
½ teaspoon cinnamon
½ teaspoon nutmeg
½ cup chopped pecans
1 cup peeled, grated apple

Preheat the oven to 350° F. Combine the maple syrup, pumpkin puree, egg, and vanilla in a blender or food processor and process until smooth. Cream the butter with an electric mixer, then stir in about half the blended mixture.

In a separate bowl, toss together the flours, baking soda, baking powder, salt, and spices. Add half of this to the creamed mixture, stirring just until blended. Stir in the rest of the pumpkin puree, followed by the remaining dry mix. Gently fold in the pecans and apple.

Spoon heaping tablespoons of the batter onto a greased baking sheet, leaving a couple of inches between them for spreading. Bake for 15 to 20 minutes, until the bottom edges just start to brown. Transfer to racks and cool.

Maple Squash Cookies
Substitute winter squash for the pumpkin.

BLONDE GINGER CUTOUT COOKIES

Preparation time: 25 minutes, plus at least 2 hours chilling time
Baking time: 10 to 12 minutes per batch   **Yield:** Depends on the way you cut it

These are a lot like gingerbread cookies. They're my kids' favorite cookie to make, and they cut them into all sorts of shapes. It is very important to chill the dough for at least 2 hours before you roll it, otherwise it will be very difficult to handle.

⅔ cup vegetable shortening
⅓ cup unsalted butter, at room temperature
1 cup maple syrup, at room temperature
1 tablespoon blackstrap molasses
½ teaspoon vanilla extract
4 cups unbleached or whole wheat flour
2 teaspoons baking soda
½ teaspoon salt
½ teaspoon ginger
¼ teaspoon nutmeg
¼ teaspoon ground cloves

Cream together the shortening and butter. Gradually beat in the maple syrup, molasses, and vanilla. Mix together the remaining ingredients and work them into the creamed mixture about 1 cup at a time. Using floured hands, divide the dough in half and wrap each half in plastic, flattening each into a disk. Chill for at least 2 hours.

Preheat the oven to 350° F. Roll the dough out, one part at a time, onto a sheet of waxed paper; make it a little less than ¼ inch thick. Cut into whatever shapes you like, transfer to a lightly greased baking sheet, and bake for 10 to 12 minutes, until the bottoms are golden. Cool briefly on the sheet, then transfer to a wire rack and finish cooling.

MAPLE GRAHAM CRACKERS

Preparation time: 20 minutes   **Baking time:** 15 minutes per batch   **Yield:** About 2 dozen crackers

For as long as I can remember, graham crackers have been a favorite food of mine. To this day, I consider a bowl of graham cracker mush (crushed graham crackers with a huge pool of light cream poured over) one of life's great comfort foods. These are much better than anything you can buy, and a whole lot of fun to make, too. The dough is easy to work with, so you can make these with kids and not end up with a terrible mess. Let them cut out animal shapes, or stegosauruses, or whatever they're into.

1½ cups whole wheat flour
1½ cups unbleached or all-purpose flour
1 teaspoon baking powder
½ teaspoon salt
⅓ cup maple syrup
⅓ cup unsalted butter, melted
1 large egg

Preheat the oven to 375° F. Combine the dry ingredients in a large mixing bowl and toss to mix. In a separate bowl, lightly beat the remaining ingredients. Make a well in the dry ingredients, then stir in the liquids with a fork. Switch to your hands and work the dough until it coheres. Roll the dough 1/8 inch thick on a large piece of waxed paper. Cut into squares, rectangles, or shapes, and pierce each once or twice with a fork. Transfer to an ungreased cookie sheet with a spatula and bake for 15 minutes. Don't let the edges brown. Transfer to a rack and cool.

WHOLE WHEAT HERMITS

Preparation time: 15 minutes   **Baking time:** About 15 minutes per batch   **Yield:** About 2½ dozen

Hermits are an old American cookie recipe, always spicy, and generally packed with nuts and dried fruit. This is the recipe my family enjoys, but there's ample room here to play with the spices, type of nuts, and so on. Purists may scowl, but a few chocolate chips might be interesting, too.

½ cup unsalted butter, at
   room temperature
½ cup maple syrup, at room
   temperature
¼ cup brown sugar, packed
1 egg
1 teaspoon baking spices (any
   combination of cinnamon,
   nutmeg, cloves, etc.)
1¼ cups whole wheat flour
1 teaspoon baking powder
Pinch salt
1 cup raisins
1 cup chopped walnuts
   or pecans
½ cup chopped dates or figs
Finely grated zest of 1 orange

Preheat the oven to 350° F. Cream the butter, gradually beating in the maple syrup, brown sugar, and egg. In a separate bowl, mix together the spices, whole wheat flour, baking powder, and salt, and work this into the creamed mixture. Stir in the remaining ingredients.

Drop slightly rounded tablespoons of dough onto a greased baking sheet, leaving a little room between them. Bake, one sheet at a time, for 15 minutes. When done, the tops will be slightly resistant to gentle finger pressure. Transfer to a rack and cool.

Pies

Roll 'em!
A few buttery crusts and
a mini-treasury of maple fillings

MAPLE APPLE PIE

Preparation time: 25 minutes, plus time to prepare pie shell
Baking time: 1¼ to 1½ hours   **Yield:** 8 to 10 servings

This is your basic maple/apple pie with a small twist, of lime, just enough to complement the maple flavor. It's a very full pie and it needs to bake a long time; don't be tempted to pull it out of the oven until the juices bubble thickly. You may substitute lemon for the lime if you'd like.

½ recipe **Whole Wheat Pastry** (page 74) **or other pie dough**
8 **cups peeled, cored, and thinly sliced cooking apples** (about 6 large ones)
½ **cup maple syrup**
1½ **tablespoons cornstarch**
½ **teaspoon finely grated lime zest**
Juice of ½ lime
2 **tablespoons butter**
Oat-Crumb Topping (page 69)

Prepare the pastry and line a 9-inch pie pan with the pastry. Form a decorative raised edge and freeze. Preheat the oven to 425° F.

Put the sliced apples in a large bowl and pour on the maple syrup. Stir to coat the slices. Sift the cornstarch over the apples, stirring as you do. Mix in the lime zest and juice. Turn the apples into the chilled crust and pat with your hands into an even mound. Dot with the butter. Butter a 12-inch square piece of foil and place it, buttered side down, over the apples, pushing it down lightly. Place the pie on a baking sheet and bake, on the center rack, for 20 minutes. Reduce the heat to 375° and cook for 10 more minutes.

After the 10 minutes, remove the foil cover and evenly distribute the Oat-Crumb Topping over the top. Bake for another 45 to 60 minutes, until the juices bubble out thickly. If the top starts to get too dark, cover loosely with the same piece of foil. Cool on a rack.

DEEP-DISH CARAMEL APPLE PIE

Preparation time: 20 minutes, plus time to prepare pie shell
Baking time: 40 minutes   **Yield:** 6 to 8 servings

This is an easy way to make a pie, because there's no bottom crust to worry about, just the top. Instead of molasses, I sometimes substitute boiled cider for an intense apple flavor.

½ recipe for Whole Wheat
　Pastry (page 74)
5 cups apples, peeled, cored,
　and sliced
½ cup maple syrup
1½ tablespoons blackstrap
　molasses
1 tablespoon unbleached or
　all-purpose flour
½ teaspoon cinnamon
½ teaspoon ground allspice
2 tablespoons unsalted butter
　or heavy cream

Prepare the Whole Wheat Pastry. Chill. Preheat the oven to 425° F.

Mix the apples, maple syrup, molasses, flour, and spices in a large mixing bowl. Turn into a 9-inch deep-dish pie pan and dot with the butter or drizzle with cream.

Roll out the dough a little larger than the pan and then place it on top of the apples, tucking it down between the apples and the sides of the dish. Poke a few vents in the crust with a fork and then bake for 10 minutes. Reduce the heat to 350° and bake for another 30 minutes. Serve warm, with whipped cream or vanilla ice cream.

SHAKER BOILED CIDER PIE

Preparation time: 20 minutes, plus time to prepare pie shell
Baking time: 40 minutes   **Yield:** 8 to 10 servings

Boiled cider is little known today, but this pie is so good it may spark a revival. The Shakers once used boiled cider as a primary sweetener because it was more economical for them than refined sugar. You can make your own boiled cider by reducing 7 cups of fresh, preservative-free cider down to 1 cup, boiling it in a large enameled or stainless pot. But I generally just buy mine by the quart from Willis & Tina Wood (RFD #2, Box 477, Springfield, VT 05016; write for a current price list). Their family has been making it for more than 100 years; they are one of the few remaining producers in this country. As for the pie, you end up with something like a rich maple-apple custard with a very thin layer of meringue on top. Possibly my favorite pie to date.

½ recipe Whole Wheat Pastry
  (page 74) or other pie dough
¾ cup boiled cider
¾ cup maple syrup
2 tablespoons unsalted butter
Pinch salt
3 large eggs, separated
⅛ teaspoon nutmeg

Prepare the pastry according to the directions and line a 9-inch pie pan with the pastry. Form a slightly raised edge and freeze. Preheat the oven to 350° F.

Gently warm the boiled cider, maple syrup, and butter in a small saucepan, just until the butter melts. Transfer to a large bowl and cool slightly. Whisk in the salt and egg yolks.

Beat the egg whites until stiff, then quickly whisk them into the liquids. Pour the filling into the chilled crust and bake, on the middle shelf, for about 40 minutes. When done, the top will be dark brown and the pie will wobble just slightly, not in waves. Cool on a rack, dusting the surface with a bit of nutmeg. Serve slightly warm or refrigerate and serve cold, which is the way I like it best. Great with vanilla ice cream or whipped cream. (Note: If you cover this pie, form a foil "tent" that doesn't touch the pie, or it will stick to the delicate meringue.)

MAPLE PECAN PIE

Preparation time: 10 minutes, plus time to prepare pie shell
Baking time: About 40 minutes   **Yield:** 8 to 10 servings

Sweet, rich, and unabashedly decadent, this should be the standard against which all pecan pies are measured. This is extraordinary in the Cornmeal Butter Pastry (page 72).

Unbaked 9-inch pie shell, well chilled
3 large eggs, at room temperature
1 cup maple syrup, at room temperature
½ cup brown sugar
Pinch salt
1 teaspoon vanilla extract
1 tablespoon flour
1⅔ cups pecan halves

Prepare the pie shell according to the directions and refrigerate. Preheat the oven to 425° F. Using an electric mixer, beat the eggs on high speed for 2 minutes. Add the remaining ingredients — except the pecans — and beat for another minute. Spread the pecans in the pie shell, then slowly pour in the liquids. Bake in the center of the oven for 10 minutes, reduce the heat to 375°, then bake for about another 30 minutes. When done, the pie will be golden, puffed, and not soupy in the middle. Cool on a rack before slicing. Break out the vanilla ice cream.

THE MAPLE SYRUP COOKBOOK

FRENCH CANADIAN MAPLE SUGAR PIE

Preparation time: 10 minutes, plus time to prepare pie shell
Baking time: 35 minutes   **Yield:** 8 to 10 servings

Another recipe from my friend Richard Sax, who credits it to a Quebec cousin-of-a-friend. He describes this, quite aptly, as something like pecan pie with a nice tart edge. It's really excellent with vanilla ice cream. Where the recipe calls for brewed tea, I like lemon herb tea.

9-inch unbaked pie shell
  (pages 70 to 75)
3 large eggs
¾ cup plus 2 tablespoons
  light brown sugar, packed
¾ cup maple syrup
6 tablespoons unsalted butter,
  melted
¼ cup brewed tea
2 tablespoons plus
  ½ teaspoon apple
  cider vinegar
Pinch salt
¾ cup coarsely chopped
  walnuts

Prepare the pie shell according to the directions and refrigerate or freeze. Preheat the oven to 450° F.

In a mixing bowl, whisk together the eggs and sugar. Add the maple syrup, butter, tea, vinegar, and salt, whisking until smooth. Stir in the walnuts. Place the pie shell on a heavy baking sheet and place on the center rack of the oven. Pour in the filling.

Bake the pie for 10 minutes, then reduce the heat to 350° and continue to bake until the center is set, about 25 minutes longer. Cool on a wire rack. Serve warm or at room temperature. This is good cold, too.

SIMPLE RHUBARB PIE

Preparation time: 15 minutes, plus time to prepare pie shell
Baking time: 60 to 70 minutes   **Yield:** 8 to 10 servings

Originally, I went through all sorts of convulsions trying to make this an "interesting" pie. I added straw-berries, cherries, and on and on, because I was afraid rhubarb would live up to its reputation as something of a culinary wallflower. Each time, the pie was great, but the subtle rhubarb and maple flavors were being crowded out by my tampering. When I finally woke up and kept just rhubarb and maple, I knew I'd hit the mark. Strike one for simplicity.

Unbaked 9-inch pie shell,
  frozen or well chilled
  (pages 70 to 75)
5 cups sliced rhubarb
  (½-inch pieces)
¼ cup sugar
⅔ cup maple syrup
1 teaspoon vanilla extract
¼ cup unbleached or all-
  purpose flour
Oat-Crumb Topping (page 69)

Prepare the pie shell according to the directions and refrigerate or freeze. Preheat the oven to 425° F. Combine the rhubarb with the sugar. Stir, then set aside for 15 minutes. Stir in the maple syrup, vanilla, and flour.

Turn the filling into the chilled pie shell and even out the top. Bake on the lower rack for 20 minutes. Remove the pie from the oven, reduce the heat to 375°, and place the pie on a baking sheet with sides (to catch the juices). Spread all the topping evenly over the pie and return it to the oven, on the middle rack. Bake for another 40 to 50 minutes until the juices bubble thickly. Cool on a rack. Slice when slightly warm.

MAPLE MINT CUSTARD PIE

Preparation time: 10 minutes, plus time to prepare pie shell
Baking time: 30 to 35 minutes   **Yield:** 8 to 10 servings

Please make this one. Words fail. My wife and I literally talked this pie into existence one evening, as we threw around ideas for cooking with mint. In my testing, I found the different fresh mints vary quite a bit in their relative mintiness. Peppermint, for instance, flavored the pie a good deal more than apple or lemon mint did. Keep this in mind when you make the pie. And if you aren't sure what type of mint you have, start with the lesser quantity of mint leaves. Serve well chilled!

9-inch partially baked Flaky
 Butter Crust pie shell
 (page 70)
⅔ cup maple syrup
¼ cup sugar
¼ to ½ cup fresh mint leaves
 (*not* packed)
1 cup heavy cream
Finely grated zest of 1 lemon
 or lime
3 large eggs, at room
 temperature

Prepare the pie shell according to the directions. Preheat the oven to 425° F. Combine the maple syrup, sugar, and mint leaves in a blender and process until smooth; you should be able to see tiny flecks, not big pieces, of mint leaves. Scrape this mixture into a medium-size saucepan, then add the cream and lemon or lime zest. Heat over medium heat, for 3 to 4 minutes, stirring occasionally. Remove from the heat.

Beat the eggs lightly in a mixing bowl. Stir about a third of the hot liquids into the eggs, wait a few seconds, then stir in the rest. Stir until smooth; don't beat it.

Carefully pour the filling into the partially baked crust. Bake on the center rack for 10 minutes, then reduce the heat to 325° and bake for another 20 to 25 minutes. The pie is done when the perimeter is slightly puffed and the center still wiggles a little. Cool on a rack to room temperature. Cover loosely with foil and chill for several hours before serving.

CRANBERRY-ORANGE PIE

Preparation time: 15 minutes   **Baking time:** About 1 hour   **Yield:** 8 to 10 servings

Some people think this pie is too heavy-handed with the cranberries. I don't, but I also don't mind telling you it tastes wonderful with apples in place of some of the cranberries. This is one of our traditional Thanksgiving pies.

Pastry for a double-crusted
   pie (pages 70 to 75)
5 cups fresh (not canned)
   cranberries
1 cup maple syrup
½ cup brown sugar, packed
1 orange, halved and sections
   removed
Finely grated zest of 1 orange
1 teaspoon ground allspice
¼ cup raisins
1½ tablespoons quick-cooking
   tapioca

Preheat the oven to 425° F. Line a 9-inch pie pan with half of the pastry. Mix together the remaining ingredients and pour into the pie shell. Slightly moisten the outer rim of the bottom crust with a damp fingertip. Roll the top crust and lay that on top, then press gently where you've moistened to seal. Trim the crusts to about ½ inch over the edge, then turn under and sculpt into an upstanding, decorative edge. Poke several steam vents in the top crust with a fork, then bake for 20 minutes. Reduce the heat to 375° and bake for about another 40 minutes, until the juices bubble thickly. Cool on a rack. Serve lukewarm or at room temperature.

SWEET POTATO PIE

Preparation time: 10 minutes, plus time to prepare pie shell
Baking time: About 45 minutes   **Yield:** 8 to 10 servings

Instead of the sweet potato puree, you could use an equal amount of winter squash, or even canned cold-pack pumpkin. This is easy and there's very little cleanup because the whole thing is mixed right in a blender.

9-inch pie shell, partially
 baked and cooled
 (pages 70 to 75)
2 cups sweet potato puree
 (bake potatoes, then
 puree flesh)
3 large eggs, at room
 temperature
½ cup maple syrup, at room
 temperature
1 cup light cream
1 tablespoon blackstrap
 molasses
1 teaspoon cinnamon
1 teaspoon ground allspice
1 teaspoon ground ginger
¼ teaspoon salt

Prepare the pie shell. Preheat the oven to 425° F. Combine all the filling ingredients in a blender or food processor and puree until smooth. Pour into the pie shell and bake for 15 minutes. Reduce the heat to 350° and bake for another 30 minutes, until a sharp knife inserted in the center of the pie emerges clean. Don't worry if the surface of the pie develops a crack; that's fine. Cool on a rack. Serve either warm, at room temperature, or chilled.

UPSIDE-DOWN SKILLET PEAR TART

Preparation time: 25 minutes, plus time to prepare pastry
Baking time: 45 minutes   **Yield:** 8 servings

This rustic tart, baked in a cast-iron skillet, is sublime. The maple-infused pears blend nicely with the crunchy cornmeal pastry — a really great combination of flavors and textures. This is just the tart to bring along to a fall potluck or party.

½ recipe Cornmeal Butter
  Pastry (page 72)
2 tablespoons unsalted butter
⅓ cup maple syrup
2 tablespoons sugar
6 large pears, halved, cored,
  and peeled

Prepare the pastry according to the directions and refrigerate. Preheat the oven to 400° F.

Melt the butter in a 9-inch or 10-inch cast-iron skillet. Stir in the maple syrup and sugar and bring to a low boil, stirring. Boil for 1½ minutes, then remove from the heat.

Arrange the pears in the skillet, rounded side down and points toward the center. Put two halves in the center, pointed in opposite directions. Any remaining halves can be sliced and interspersed on top of the others. Try to keep the top level of the pears even, but don't lose any sleep over it — it's bound to be jagged.

Roll the cornmeal pastry into a 12-inch circle. Lay it on top of the pears and tuck the edge down between the pears and the side of the skillet. Make 2 or 3 wide slashes in the crust, so steam can escape. Bake for 45 minutes.

Remove the tart from the oven and let cool for 10 minutes. Place a plate directly on top of the crust. Ideally, it should just fit the skillet. Quickly invert the tart, tilting it slightly away from you to avoid getting hot syrup on your hands and arms. (This is best done over a sink.) Let cool at least 15 minutes before cutting. It will probably be a little juicy; that's fine. Any juice can be spooned back over the pears to glaze them.

OAT-CRUMB TOPPING

Preparation time: 5 minutes   **Yield:** About 1½ cups (enough for 1 pie)

This is a good, general purpose crunchy topping for pies, bars, crumbles, crisps, and all those wonderful sweet things. It can be made with either white or light brown sugar. The disadvantage to the white sugar is that it tends to brown quicker. But you can prevent excessive browning by loosely covering with foil.

½ cup unbleached or all-
   purpose flour
½ cup white or brown sugar
⅓ cup rolled oats
   (non-instant)
Pinch salt
Pinch cinnamon
4 tablespoons cold, unsalted
   butter, cut into ¼-inch
   pieces

Combine the flour, sugar, oats, salt, and cinnamon in a large bowl. Toss to mix. Cut the cold butter into the dry ingredients until the mixture is uniform and somewhat gravelly in texture. It shouldn't get to the point where it all starts to clump together; stop if that happens. Store, refrigerated and covered, until you are ready to use it. Freeze for longer storage.

FLAKY BUTTER CRUST

Preparation time: 15 minutes, plus chilling time
Baking time: Varies with pie   **Yield:** One double-crusted 9-inch pie or two 9-inch pie shells

Everybody has their own special recipe for pie crust; this is one of mine. Made with both butter and a little vegetable shortening, it is flavorful and flaky. The little bit of lemon juice tenderizes the crust, so it's noticeably delicate. If you are using this for a top and bottom crust, make one half slightly larger than the other. Because so many of the pies in this book go from freezer to oven, it is important to use a metal pie pan.

2½ cups unbleached or all-
  purpose flour
½ teaspoon salt
12 tablespoons cold unsalted
  butter, cut into ¼-inch
  pieces
¼ cup vegetable shortening
1 tablespoon sugar
1 large egg, cold
2 tablespoons ice cold water
1 tablespoon lemon juice or
  vinegar

Combine the flour and salt in a large mixing bowl and toss to mix. Cut the butter and vegetable shortening into the flour until the butter is evenly distributed, with pieces of fat no larger than split peas. Add the sugar and toss with your fingers to incorporate.

Beat together the egg, water, and lemon juice or vinegar with a fork. Drizzle half of this liquid over the flour, tossing the mixture with a fork. Add the rest of the liquid, tossing and blending as you pour. Work the mixture briefly with your fork, then try to pack the dough together, like a snowball. If dry spots remain, use wet fingertips to pull them into the ball of dough. Divide the dough in half and flatten each half into a disk about ½ inch thick. Wrap each half in plastic and refrigerate for at least 30 minutes.

To roll the dough, place a 12-inch square piece of waxed paper on a countertop. Place half of the dough on it and roll the disk into a circle 12 inches in diameter. Dust the dough's surface with a little flour, if needed, to prevent the dough from sticking to your pin. Flip the waxed paper over, inverting the rolled dough over the pie pan, then peel off the paper. Tuck the dough into the pan, without stretching it.

If you are making a pie shell, trim the overhang to an even ½ inch, then tuck the overhang under, sculpting the edge into an upstanding ridge. Form a decorative edge, if desired, cover with plastic, and freeze.

If you are making a double-crusted pie, roll out half as for a pie shell, but do not trim. Cover with plastic, and refrigerate while you roll the top crust. Fill the pie, run a moistened fingertip around the rim of the bottom crust and lay the top sheet of dough over the filling. Press down slightly where you've moistened the edge, to seal. Trim the overhang to an even ½ inch, then tuck it under, sculpting the edge into an upstanding ridge. Form a decorative edge, if desired, and poke 3 or 4 steam vents in the top crust with the tines of a fork. Bake as directed.

To partially prebake a pie shell, preheat the oven to 425° F. Line the frozen shell with a 12-inch square of foil, tucking it into the contours of the pan. Spread about 2 cups of dried rice or beans in the bottom and slightly up the sides of the foil. Bake the crust in the lower part of the oven for 15 minutes, then carefully lift out the foil and beans. Prick the bottom several times with a fork, so steam can escape. Reduce the heat to 375° and bake for another 10 minutes. Cool on a rack.

To fully prebake a pie shell, proceed as above, but bake the crust for about 20 minutes after lowering the heat, until evenly browned all over.

CORNMEAL BUTTER PASTRY

Preparation time: 15 minutes
Baking time: Varies with pie   **Yield:** One double-crusted 9-inch pie or two 9-inch pie shell

One of the advantages of this earthy pastry is that the cornmeal helps to break up the gluten structure —gluten being the part of the wheat that forms elastic strands — and therefore this has almost no tendency to shrink. So this is a very good choice for prebaked pie or tart shells. The dough is easiest to roll after a brief (10 to 15 minutes) chilling. You really have to try this with the Upside-Down Skillet Pear Tart (page 66).

1¾ cups unbleached or all-purpose flour
¾ cup cornmeal, preferably stone-ground
¾ teaspoon salt
14 tablespoons cold unsalted butter, cut into ¼-inch pieces
About 6 tablespoons ice cold water

Combine the flour, cornmeal, and salt in a large mixing bowl and toss to mix. Add the butter and spend a few seconds breaking it up with your fingertips. Cut the butter into the dry mixture, until everything is about the size of split peas or a little smaller. Sprinkle in half the water, stirring with a fork. Gradually add the remaining water, stirring and tossing, until the mixture can be collected into a cohesive mass; don't be afraid to work it a bit with your fingers to get it to cohere.

Divide the dough in half, flattening each piece into a ½-inch-thick disk. Wrap each in plastic and refrigerate, if you are not rolling it right away.

To roll the dough, place a 12-inch square piece of waxed paper on a countertop. Place half of the dough on it and roll the disk into a circle 12 inches in diameter. Dust the dough's surface with a little flour, if needed, to prevent the dough from sticking to your pin. Flip the waxed paper over, inverting the rolled dough over the pie pan, then peel off the paper. Tuck the dough into the pan, without stretching it.

If you are making a pie shell, trim the overhang to an even ½ inch, then tuck the overhang under, sculpting the edge into an upstanding ridge. Form a decorative edge, if desired, cover with plastic, and freeze.

If you are making a double-crusted pie, roll out half as for a pie shell, but do not trim. Cover with plastic, and refrigerate while you roll the top crust. Fill the pie, run a moistened fingertip around the rim of the bottom crust and lay the top sheet of dough over the filling. Press down slightly where you've moistened the edge, to seal. Trim the overhang to an even ½ inch, then tuck it under, sculpting the edge into an upstanding ridge. Form a decorative edge, if desired, and poke 3 or 4 steam vents in the top crust with the tines of a fork. Bake as directed.

To partially prebake a pie shell, preheat the oven to 425° F. Line the frozen shell with a 12-inch square of foil, tucking it into the contours of the pan. Spread about 2 cups of dried rice or beans in the bottom and slightly up the sides of the foil. Bake the crust in the lower part of the oven for 15 minutes, then carefully lift out the foil and beans. Prick the bottom several times with a fork, so steam can escape. Reduce the heat to 375° and bake for another 10 minutes. Cool on a rack.

To fully prebake a pie shell, proceed as above, but bake the crust for about 20 minutes after lowering the heat, until evenly browned all over.

WHOLE WHEAT PASTRY

Preparation time: 10 minutes   **Yield:** One double-crusted 9-inch pie or two 9-inch pie shells

This half whole wheat pie dough is a good way to acquaint yourself with whole grain pastry. It's no more difficult to handle than any other pastry, especially if you roll it directly onto a sheet of waxed paper. I've included this because I think the earthy, wheat flavor is a natural sidekick to any maple-sweetened pie.

1¼ cups whole wheat flour
1¼ cups unbleached or all-purpose flour
½ teaspoon salt
½ cup cold vegetable shortening
6 tablespoons cold unsalted butter, cut into ¼-inch pieces
4 to 5 tablespoons ice cold water

In a large mixing bowl, combine the whole wheat and unbleached flours with the salt; stir well. Cut in the shortening and butter until the mixture resembles a very coarse meal. Sprinkle on the ice water, 1 tablespoon at a time, tossing with a fork after each addition. When the dough is able to be massed together, like a snowball, divide it in half and form 2 balls. Flatten each into a ½-inch-thick disk. Cover with plastic wrap and refrigerate for at least 30 minutes before rolling out. If it remains in the cold for more than 2 hours, let it sit at room temperature for 5 to 10 minutes before rolling.

To roll the dough, place a 12-inch square piece of waxed paper on a countertop. Place half of the dough on it and roll the disk into a circle 12 inches in diameter. Dust the dough's surface with a little flour, if needed, to prevent the dough from sticking to your pin. Flip the waxed paper over, inverting the rolled dough over the pie pan, then peel off the paper. Tuck the dough into the pan, without stretching it.

If you are making a pie shell, trim the overhang to an even ½ inch, then tuck the overhang under, sculpting the edge into an upstanding ridge. Form a decorative edge, if desired, cover with plastic, and freeze.

If you are making a double-crusted pie, roll out half as for a pie shell, but do not trim. Cover with plastic, and refrigerate while you roll the top crust. Fill the pie, run a moistened fingertip around the rim of the bottom crust and lay the top sheet of dough over the filling. Press down slightly where you've moistened the edge, to seal. Trim the overhang to an even ½ inch, then tuck it under, sculpting the edge into an upstanding ridge. Form a decorative edge, if desired, and poke 3 or 4 steam vents in the top crust with the tines of a fork. Bake as directed.

To partially prebake a pie shell, preheat the oven to 425° F. Line the frozen shell with a 12-inch square of foil, tucking it into the contours of the pan. Spread about 2 cups of dried rice or beans in the bottom and slightly up the sides of the foil. Bake the crust in the lower part of the oven for 15 minutes, then carefully lift out the foil and beans. Prick the bottom several times with a fork, so steam can escape. Reduce the heat to 375° and bake for another 10 minutes. Cool on a rack.

To fully prebake a pie shell, proceed as above, but bake the crust for about 20 minutes after lowering the heat, until evenly browned all over.

Cakes & Breads

Wherein we bake and steam our way
through all manner of grainy pleasures

STEAMED BOSTON BROWN BREAD

Preparation time: 15 minutes
Steaming time: 2 hours   **Yield:** 2 round loaves, 8 to 10 slices each

Traditionally, this bread is made with molasses, not maple syrup; but once you've tasted this version, I think you'll excuse the liberties I've taken. Some folks don't like you to tamper with tradition. I can remember publishing a recipe for Boston brown bread in a magazine, only to have some irate fellow write to the editor, blasting me for instructing readers to cut this with a sharp, serrated knife. Of course, the only correct way to slice it, this fellow maintained, was with twine — you wrap it around the loaf and pull the ends. Oh well, whether you use a knife, twine, or dental floss, do serve it with soft cream cheese. Some people like to soak the raisins in a little rum beforehand.

1 cup whole wheat flour
1 cup cornmeal
1 cup rye flour
1 teaspoon baking powder
1 teaspoon baking soda
1 teaspoon salt
2 cups buttermilk
1 cup maple syrup
1 cup raisins

Butter two 1-pound coffee cans, including the insides of their plastic lids. Place a trivet, large enough to support both cans, in the bottom of a wide, deep pot. Add hot water to about 3 inches above the trivet. Place the pot on a burner over medium heat.

Toss together the dry ingredients in a large mixing bowl. In a separate bowl, beat the buttermilk and maple syrup. Make a well in the dry ingredients, add the liquids, and stir just to blend. Fold in the raisins. Divide the batter evenly between the cans and put on the lids. Wrap a large piece of foil over each lid and secure with a heavy rubber band or twine. Put the cans in the water; the level should rise about half to two-thirds the way up the sides of the cans. Cover the pot with its lid if it will fit, or fashion a foil tent.

Bring the water to a boil. Reduce the heat and simmer for approximately 2 hours. Check the water level once or twice, and replenish with boiling hot water if it falls below the halfway mark. The bread is done when a tester, inserted deeply, emerges clean. Remove the bread from the cans. Place on a lightly greased baking sheet and put them in a preheated 350° F. oven for 5 minutes to dry the outside surfaces. Serve warm or cool on a rack.

BETTER-THAN-THE-MONKS' FRUITCAKE

Preparation time: 1 1/2 hours total   **Baking time:** 1 to 3 hours   **Yield:** Varies by size of pans

Several years ago I wrote an article on mail-order fruitcakes, and in the process sampled maybe a dozen from assorted monasteries, bakeries, and other entrepreneurs. Some were very good, some were awful, but the best by far — when all the tasting was said and done — was the following maple fruitcake I've been making for years. It's difficult to give you an exact yield. There's roughly 22 cups of batter here. That's enough for 2 large tube pans, 4 to 5 medium-size loaf pans, or 10 to 12 smaller aluminum pans. I like to make it in the latter and give them away to a lot of different people at Christmas. (I think people can O.D. on a big fruitcake.) You have to start this a day or so ahead, mixing up the nut and fruit mixture.

Nut and Fruit Mixture
- 12 cups assorted dried fruit (raisins, dates, prunes, apricots, etc.)
- 8 cups assorted nuts (walnuts, pecans, almonds, but no peanuts)
- 2 tablespoons finely grated lemon or orange zest
- 4 teaspoons assorted spices (cinnamon, cloves, nutmeg, etc.)
- 2 cups maple syrup
- 2 cups rum, brandy, or fruit juice

Cake
- 2 cups unsalted butter, at room temperature
- 2 cups light brown sugar, packed
- 8 large eggs, at room temperature
- 1 tablespoon vanilla extract

A day or so ahead of baking, cut or break the fruit and nuts into edible-size pieces; they don't have to be real small. Put them in a very large bowl and stir in the zest, spices, maple syrup, and spirits or fruit juice. Set aside and keep tightly covered, out of mouse range. Stir periodically. It isn't necessary to refrigerate it.

To make the cake, preheat the oven to 275° F. Lightly grease all your pans and line them with waxed paper.

Cream the butter with an electric mixer. Add the brown sugar and continue to beat until light and fluffy. Add the eggs, one at a time, beating well after each addition. Add the vanilla.

In a separate bowl, stir together the flour, salt, and baking powder. Stir into the creamed mixture, 1 cup at a time, blending just until smooth. Combine the batter with the fruit and nut mixture, including any juice left in the bowl. Mix with your hands because that's the only good way to do it. Fill the prepared pans about three-quarters full and put them in the oven. The large cakes will take as long as 3 hours to bake, the small ones about an hour, and the medium-size ones 1½ to 2 hours; check them with a cake tester.

Remove the cakes to a wire rack, but keep them in the pans. When they are still barely warm, remove them from the pans, and peel off the waxed paper. Brush with spirits (rum or brandy). After several hours, wrap the cakes in muslin, brush with more spirits,

4 cups unbleached or all-
purpose flour (may be part
whole wheat)
2 teaspoons salt
2 teaspoons baking powder
Additional rum or brandy for
brushing on finished cakes

and store in plastic bags or tins. Every few days, reapply the spirits. Store in a cool spot. These can be eaten after several days or stored for many months in an airtight container.

DEANNA'S EGGLESS APPLESAUCE YOGURT CAKE

Preparation time: 20 minutes   **Baking time:** 45 minutes   **Yield:** About 15 servings

My friend, Deanna, whose recipe this is, knows her way around the kitchen. Like me, she loves to bake, and this egg-free maple cake is solid proof of her prowess. I swear, you'd never know the egg was missing. It's soft and tender, spiced just right, and the yogurt gives the cake a pleasant after-tang. Deanna uses whole wheat pastry flour, available in health food stores, but I've used regular whole wheat and it comes out just fine.

¾ cup unsalted butter,
    at room temperature
1 cup maple syrup, at room
    temperature
1 cup applesauce
½ cup plain yogurt
2 teaspoons vanilla extract
1 tablespoon water
2½ cups whole wheat pastry
    flour
1 tablespoon baking powder
1 teaspoon cinnamon
½ teaspoon salt
¼ teaspoon nutmeg
¾ cup finely chopped walnuts

Preheat the oven to 350° F. Butter a 7½-inch by 12-inch baking pan.

Cream the butter with an electric mixer, slowly drizzling in the maple syrup. Mix in the applesauce, yogurt, vanilla, and water.

Combine the whole wheat flour, baking powder, cinnamon, salt, and nutmeg in a separate bowl, and toss to mix. Add the dry ingredients to the creamed in several stages, stirring just to blend after each addition. Turn the batter into the prepared pan, then sprinkle on the nuts. Bake for about 45 minutes, until a tester comes out clean, and the cake pulls away from the sides of the pan. Cool in the pan and serve lukewarm or at room temperature.

MINNESOTA KATE'S COSMIC CARROT CAKE

Preparation time: 25 minutes   **Baking time:** 35 to 40 minutes   **Yield:** 15 or more servings

Minnesota Kate didn't invent this recipe, but she liked it so much I named it after her. She's not the only one who has liked it. Several years ago, when my friends Mike and Nancy got married, I multiplied this recipe by about a zillion and made it into a multitiered wedding cake for 200. And they all liked it. I think the maple, whole wheat flour, and ground almonds are what give this cake its special character and appeal.

Cake
4 large eggs
1 cup maple syrup, at room temperature
1¼ cups light vegetable oil
½ cup sour cream
1 tablespoon lemon juice
1 teaspoon vanilla extract
1 teaspoon almond extract
1 cup whole wheat flour
1 cup unbleached or all-purpose flour
1½ cups finely ground almonds (almost like an almond meal; use a blender or food processor)
1 tablespoon baking powder
1 teaspoon cinnamon
1 teaspoon ground allspice
½ teaspoon salt
Finely grated zest of 1 orange
2 cups grated carrots
1 cup raisins

Preheat the oven to 350° F. Butter a 9-inch by 13-inch baking pan. Using an electric mixer, beat the eggs on high speed for 1 minute. Continue to beat, gradually adding the maple syrup, oil, sour cream, lemon juice, and extracts.

In a separate bowl, sift together the flours. Then stir in the almonds, baking powder, spices, salt, and orange zest. Make a well in the dry ingredients, then add the liquids all at once. Stir just until smooth, then fold in the carrots and raisins. Scrape into the prepared pan and bake for 35 to 40 minutes, until a tester emerges clean. Cool in the pan, on a rack, then frost.

Cosmic Frosting

12 ounces cream cheese,
   at room temperature
⅔ cup maple syrup, at room
   temperature
1 teaspoon vanilla extract
1 teaspoon finely grated
   lemon zest

To make the frosting, beat the cream cheese with an electric mixer until soft and fluffy. Gradually add the maple syrup, vanilla, and lemon zest. Ice the cake when it has cooled.

LEMON MAPLE ZUCCHINI BREAD

Preparation time: 15 minutes
Baking time: 50 to 60 minutes   **Yield:** 1 very large loaf or 2 smaller loaves

I've come to think of zucchini bread recipes as sort of the equivalent of public service messages you hear on the radio: They're helpful, even though we have become indifferent to them by overexposure. But I do think this moist, maple variation is a particularly good one and definitely worth a try next time the annual summer zucchini invasion rolls around.

3 large eggs
1 cup maple syrup
½ cup vegetable oil
1 teaspoon vanilla extract
Finely grated zest of 1 lemon
1½ cups grated zucchini or
   yellow summer squash
1½ cups unbleached or all-
   purpose flour
1 cup whole wheat flour
1 tablespoon baking powder
½ teaspoon salt

Preheat the oven to 350° F. Butter one large (9-inch by 5-inch) or two medium-size (7½-inch by 4-inch) loaf pans and set aside.

Beat the eggs with an electric mixer for 2 minutes. Gradually add the maple syrup, oil, vanilla, and lemon zest. Stir in the squash. Mix the dry ingredients in a separate bowl, make a well in the center, then stir in the liquids. Blend just until smooth, then turn into the prepared pans. Bake for 50 to 60 minutes, until a tester comes out clean. Cool in the pans for 5 to 10 minutes, then remove them and cool on a rack.

WHOLE WHEAT & OAT YEASTED LOAVES

Preparation time: 20 minutes, plus 2 to 3 hours rising time
Baking time: 45 minutes   **Yield:** 2 large loaves

It takes a considerable amount of maple syrup to get any kind of clear maple flavor at all from a yeasted bread. I do have a trick, however, for accenting the maple flavor when I use this recipe to make rolls, as I often do. What I do is brush the rolls after they have risen with a mixture of 1 tablespoon melted butter and 1 tablespoon maple syrup, which not only clarifies the maple flavor but gives the rolls a dark, glossy sheen. Don't do this on the large loaves, however, because the tops will burn during the longer baking time. This makes an excellent toasting loaf.

1¼ cups milk
¾ cup buttermilk
¾ cup rolled oats
   (non-instant)
⅓ cup lukewarm water
1 tablespoon active dry yeast
½ cups whole wheat flour
5 tablespoons unsalted butter,
   softened
⅔ cup maple syrup
1 egg, lightly beaten
1 tablespoon salt
Approximately 3 cups
   unbleached or all-purpose
   flour

In a saucepan, warm the milk and buttermilk until hot to the touch. Put the oats in a large mixing bowl and pour the warm milk over them. Set aside. Pour the water into a separate, small bowl and sprinkle on the yeast. When the oat liquid cools to about skin temperature, stir in the dissolved yeast. Using a heavy wooden spoon, stir 2 cups of the whole wheat flour into the liquid, beating hard for 1 minute. Cover this sponge and let rise for 60 minutes.

Beat the soft butter into the sponge, followed by the maple syrup, egg, and salt. Stir in the remaining 1½ cups whole wheat flour. Cover and let rise for 10 minutes.

Now start stirring in the unbleached flour, about ½ cup at a time, until the dough becomes too stiff to beat. Then turn the dough out onto a floured surface. Begin kneading, gently at first, using flour as needed, to prevent sticking. Knead a good 10 minutes, until the dough is smooth and fairly elastic. Place in a large, lightly oiled bowl and turn to coat the entire surface. Cover, and let rise until doubled in bulk, about 1 hour.

Punch the dough down, knead briefly, and divide it in half. Shape the dough into loaves and place the loaves in 2 large, buttered loaf pans. (I like to roll it out into a tapered rectangle, the taper toward me, and roll the dough up like a carpet; this puts adequate tension on the dough and gives the top a nice, rounded appearance.) Cover and set aside, to double in bulk, 30 to 45 minutes.

Preheat the oven to 375° F. when the loaves are almost doubled.

When fully doubled, bake the loaves for about 45 minutes, until all surfaces are nicely browned. Remove the loaves from their pans and cool on a rack. Store in plastic bags.

Note: To make dinner rolls, break off golf ball-size pieces of dough and shape into rounds. Place, almost touching, on a buttered baking sheet. Let rise, brush with glaze (see recipe introduction), and bake for 25 to 30 minutes.

PINEAPPLE UPSIDE-DOWN SPICE CAKE

Preparation time: 25 minutes   **Baking time:** 30 minutes   **Yield:** 8 servings

This is incredibly good: pineapple slices paired with the Buttermilk Maple Spice Cake. I love the mapley-goo stuff that runs between the pineapple slices, especially near the edge, where it turns to goo/crunch. Instead of pineapple, sometimes you might want to try fresh apple rings, or peeled peach or pear halves, flat side down in the pan.

1 recipe Buttermilk Maple
    Spice Cake (page 86)
7 canned pineapple slices
    (rings)
4 tablespoons unsalted butter
⅓ cup maple syrup
⅓ cup sugar

Preheat the oven to 350° F. Prepare the cake recipe, but do not mix the wet and dry ingredients together yet. Blot the pineapple slices dry and set them aside.

Melt the butter in a 9-inch or 10-inch cast-iron skillet. Stir in the maple syrup and bring to a boil. Boil for 1 minute, stir in the sugar, and boil for 1 minute more. Remove from the heat and arrange the pineapple slices in the pan — 1 in the center and the rest around it. Set aside.

Make a well in the dry cake ingredients and add the liquids. Stir, just until blended. Pour the cake batter over the pineapple slices. Bake for 30 minutes. Remove from oven and let sit for 2 minutes. Put a plate on top of the cake and invert. Serve hot or warm, with whipped cream or vanilla ice cream.

BUTTERMILK MAPLE SPICE CAKE

Preparation time: 15 minutes   **Baking time:** 30 minutes   **Yield:** 9 to 12 servings

In general, I like to make simple cakes, such as this one. The spices can be increased, but don't go too heavy on the spice or you'll mask the subtle maple flavor. A good snack item for brown baggers or for dessert, with whipped cream.

1 cup unbleached or all-
   purpose flour
½ cup whole wheat flour
1 teaspoon baking powder
1 teaspoon baking soda
½ teaspoon cinnamon
½ teaspoon ginger
¼ teaspoon nutmeg
¼ teaspoon ground cloves
½ teaspoon salt
Pinch cayenne
2 large eggs, lightly beaten
⅔ cup buttermilk
½ cup maple syrup
⅓ cup vegetable oil
1 tablespoon blackstrap
   molasses

Preheat the oven to 350° F. Butter an 8½-inch by 8½-inch baking pan. Sift together all of the dry ingredients into a large mixing bowl. Set aside. In another bowl, blend the remaining ingredients. Make a well in the dry mixture and stir in the liquids, just until smooth; do not beat. Pour the batter into the prepared pan and bake for 30 minutes, until a tester emerges clean. Cool in the pan.

TAWNY MAPLE CHEESECAKE

Preparation time: 25 minutes   **Baking time:** 1 hour   **Yield:** 16 servings

Having spent a fair chunk of my youth cruising the New Jersey diner circuit, I know a thing or two about cheesecakes. I know, for instance, that I like mine light, moist, and creamy — and hold the canned fruit toppings please. That's why I like this one. This is wonderful with a cup of coffee, about an hour after dinner (or before breakfast).

1¼ cups fine graham
  cracker crumbs
5 tablespoons sugar
5 tablespoons unsalted
  butter, at room temperature
¾ cup maple syrup
¼ cup heavy cream
1½ pounds cream cheese, at
  room temperature
3 large eggs, at room
  temperature
1½ cups sour cream, at
  room temperature
1½ teaspoons vanilla extract

Combine the cracker crumbs and 1 tablespoon of the sugar in a mixing bowl with the soft butter. Rub together thoroughly, then press into the bottom of a 9-inch springform pan. Freeze. Preheat the oven to 350° F.

In a medium-size saucepan, bring the maple syrup to a boil over medium heat. Boil for 3 minutes, remove from the heat, and stir in the cold cream. Scrape into a bowl and refrigerate.

Using a heavy-duty electric mixer, cream the cream cheese until light and fluffy. Add the remaining 4 tablespoons sugar and beat briefly, then add the eggs, one at a time. When the maple syrup is no longer warm to the touch, gradually beat it in also, followed by the sour cream and vanilla. Scrape into the chilled pan and bake for 1 hour. Carefully transfer to a rack and cool thoroughly. Cover, then chill for at least 6 hours before serving.

More Desserts & Sweets

A heavenly rich assortment
of puddings, pastries, and ices
wherein the pleasure principle is further explored

CRÈME BRÛLÉE

Preparation time: 20 minutes, plus overnight chilling
Baking time: 1 hour   **Yield:** 5 to 6 servings

Crème Brûlée, the king of custards, is very popular these days. It has probably done more recently to broaden the waistlines of restaurant goers in this country than any other dessert. This version, though slightly less rich than most, is taking its toll on my own mid-region. You must begin this the day before you plan to serve it.

6 egg yolks
½ cup maple syrup
2 cups light cream
1 cup heavy cream
1 teaspoon *pure* vanilla
    extract
6 tablespoons light brown
    sugar

Preheat the oven to 325° F. Bring about 4 cups of water to a boil and reserve.

Very lightly whisk the egg yolks and maple syrup together. Set aside. Scald the heavy and light creams in a heavy-bottomed saucepan.

Gradually stir the hot cream into the yolk/maple syrup mixture, until blended. Do not beat it or the finished texture will be grainy. Stir in the vanilla. Ladle into individual, ovenproof custard cups or ramekins of about ¾-cup capacity, filling almost to the rim.

Place the cups in a large, shallow casserole, then carefully pour in the boiled water until it reaches about halfway up the sides of the cups. Take care not to splash water in the cups. Cover loosely with foil, then bake for 1 hour. The centers will still seem a little wobbly, but they will firm as the custards cool. Cool to room temperature, cover with plastic, then refrigerate overnight.

About an hour before serving, remove the cups from the refrigerator. Sieve 1 tablespoon of brown sugar directly on top of each custard, spreading it evenly with a fork. Put the cups in a shallow casserole, then pour in enough ice water to come halfway up the sides of the cups. Turn on the broiler and broil the custard close to the heat, until the brown sugar bubbles and darkens; watch carefully, or it will burn. Cool and serve right away in the cups. Or rechill until serving.

BAKED CUSTARD

Preparation time: 10 minutes   **Baking time:** 50 minutes   **Yield:** About 6 servings

Baked custard is one of the simplest things in the world to make, and a real crowd-pleaser when it is made with maple syrup. One thing to remember about custard is not to beat it excessively, which only makes the finished texture grainy. Just stir everything together nice and easy, then ladle into custard cups. I think the maple flavor comes out best when this is served cold, but warm custard has its proponents, too.

4 large eggs, lightly beaten
½ cup maple syrup
1 teaspoon vanilla extract
¼ teaspoon salt
3 cups milk, heated just to the boiling point

Preheat the oven to 350° F. Bring about 4 cups of water to a boil and reserve.

With a whisk, gently blend together the eggs, maple syrup, vanilla, and salt. Slowly stir in the hot milk. Ladle into custard cups, filling each to within ¼ inch of the rim. Place the cups in a large, shallow casserole and carefully pour the boiled water into the pan, until it comes about halfway up the cups. Bake for about 50 minutes, until the edges seem set but the middle a bit wiggly; they'll finish cooking as they cool. Serve warm, or cool to room temperature, cover, and chill.

CREAMY MAPLE MOCHA PUDDING

Preparation time: 20 minutes   **Yield:** 4 to 5 servings

Classic comfort food, this, the sort of thing we all cherished as kids and now secretly yearn for since the onset of rampant mousse-ification. You get a rich maple flavor here, intensified by the coffee and cocoa — a winning team effort. I ladle this into small glass dessert bowls or goblets and serve with plenty of whipped cream.

3 tablespoons cornstarch
1 tablespoon powdered
   instant coffee or powdered
   instant espresso
1 teaspoon unsweetened
   cocoa
Pinch salt
3 egg yolks
3 cups milk
½ cup maple syrup
1 tablespoon unsalted butter,
   cut into pieces
1 teaspoon vanilla extract

Combine the cornstarch, coffee, cocoa, and salt in a large, heavy-bottomed pot and whisk to mix. In a mixing bowl, whisk the egg yolks slightly, then add the milk and maple syrup. Stir into the pot and begin to heat over medium-high heat.

Gradually bring the mixture to a boil, stirring gently but constantly with a rubber spatula. Be sure to scrape the sides as you stir. When the mixture finally comes to a boil, boil for 1 minute, stirring. Remove from the heat and stir in the butter and vanilla.

Ladle into 4 or 5 individual serving bowls. To prevent a skin from forming, place a piece of waxed paper — cut to size — on top of each. Cool, then chill for several hours before serving.

STEAMED WINTER SQUASH AND DATE NUT PUDDING

Preparation time: 30 minutes
Steaming time: 1¾ to 2 hours   **Yield:** 12 to 16 servings

This is a treasured recipe. It's beautiful to look at. The ingredients are wholesome. And the flavor is divine. Plus, it has that old-fashioned appeal. It can actually be served as a bread, with meals; for breakfast, slathered with soft cream cheese perhaps; or as a dessert, with lightly sweetened whipped cream. Any way, you'll adore this. If you cannot find an 8-cup pudding mold with central tube locally, write to F.H. Gillingham & Sons, 16 Elm St., Woodstock, VT 05091. They stock an excellent selection of cookware. This can, alternatively, be steamed in two 1-pound coffee cans.

3 cups butternut or other winter squash (not spaghetti) or pumpkin, peeled and diced (¾-inch to 1-inch pieces)
5 tablespoons unsalted butter, at room temperature
1 cup maple syrup
2 large eggs, lightly beaten
Finely grated zest of 1 lemon
1 cup cornmeal, preferably stone-ground
1 cup whole wheat flour
1 cup unbleached or all-purpose flour
2½ teaspoons baking powder
1½ teaspoons salt
1 teaspoon cinnamon
½ cup chopped pitted dates or raisins
½ cup chopped walnuts or pecans

Put the winter squash in a saucepan and cover with about a quart of water. Bring to a boil, cover, and reduce the heat to an active simmer. Cook for about 20 minutes, until very tender.

Drain the squash briefly in a colander, then transfer to a blender or food processor. Add 4 tablespoons of the soft butter and puree until smooth; you should have about 1½ cups of puree. Scrape into a mixing bowl, then whisk in the maple syrup, eggs, and lemon zest. Set aside.

Butter the insides and lid of an 8-cup pudding mold or two 1-pound coffee cans, using the remaining tablespoon of soft butter. Set aside. Put about 3½ inches of water in a large, tall pot; ideally, it should be tall enough to accommodate the mold standing on a trivet, with the cover on. (If not, a snug foil cover will do.) Place a trivet in the center of the pot, cover, and bring the water to a boil.

Combine the cornmeal, flours, baking powder, salt, and cinnamon in a bowl. Toss to mix. Make a well in the dry ingredients and add the liquids. Stir just until blended, then fold in the dates and nuts. Spoon the batter into the prepared mold and put on the lid. (If using coffee cans, put on plastic lids, then press a double layer of foil over the tops and secure with heavy twine.)

When the water comes to a boil, reduce the heat to an active simmer. Place the mold or cans on the trivet; the water should come at least halfway, but no more than two-thirds up the sides. Cover the pot and steam for 1¾ to 2 hours, until the top is springy to the touch and a cake tester emerges clean. Remove the lid(s) and cool on a rack for 5 minutes. Invert onto a rack. Cool for at least 15 minutes before slicing. This can be served warm or at room temperature, thinly sliced with a serrated knife. Cool thoroughly before storing in a plastic bag.

INDIAN PUDDING

Preparation time: 20 minutes   **Baking time:** 2½ hours   **Yield:** About 8 servings

Indian pudding, from what I understand, is the oldest New England dessert on record. One taste of this soft, creamy maple version and you'll quickly understand why this dessert has a history behind it. A number of restaurants have built their reputations on their versions of Indian pudding, including the famous Durgin Park in Boston. I've had theirs; this one's better.

5 cups milk
⅔ cup cornmeal
½ teaspoon salt
1 cup maple syrup
1 tablespoon blackstrap
 molasses
4 tablespoons unsalted butter
½ teaspoon ginger
½ teaspoon cinnamon
1 cup raisins or finely chopped
 dates

Preheat the oven to 300° F. Butter a shallow, 9-inch by 13-inch casserole.

In a large, heavy-bottomed pot, heat the milk over medium heat. Slowly sprinkle in the cornmeal, whisking as you do so. Switch to a wooden spoon and continue to cook and stir for about 10 minutes, until the mixture has thickened. Reduce the heat, add the remaining ingredients, and stir for another minute or two. Pour into the prepared baking dish and bake for 2½ hours. Serve warm, with plenty of vanilla ice cream.

MAPLE BAKLAVA

Preparation time: 40 to 45 minutes   **Baking time:** 1½ hours   **Yield:** About 3 dozen pieces

It is almost impossible to find good versions of baklava outside of a major city. So rather than move to a metropolitan area, I decided to master the intricacies of this flaky Greek pastry at home, using maple syrup. Here it is. You'll need to find packaged phyllo dough, which is widely available in grocery and health food stores. The brand I buy comes in large sheets which, when cut in half, fit beautifully into a 9-inch by 13-inch pan. I encourage you to read the package instructions for working with phyllo because there are a few little tricks. This is one sweet treat, a real cavity screamer.

Syrup
1½ cups maple syrup
¼ cup honey
⅔ cup water
1 tablespoon lemon juice

Filling
4 cups chopped walnuts
1 teaspoon cinnamon
½ teapoon ground cloves
Finely grated zest of 1 lemon
½ cup warm honey
24 sheets phyllo dough, each about 9½ inches by 13½ inches
14 tablespoons unsalted butter, melted

To make the syrup, combine the maple syrup, ¼ cup honey, water, and lemon juice in a saucepan. Heat almost to the boiling point. Reduce the heat and barely simmer for 10 minutes. Cool to room temperature.

To make the filling, mix the walnuts, cinnamon, cloves, lemon zest, and ½ cup warm honey in a mixing bowl. Set aside. Butter a 9-inch by 13-inch glass, stainless steel, or enameled baking pan. Place 12 sheets of phyllo dough in the pan, buttering each sheet with a little melted butter. Spread half the filling evenly on the top sheet. Cover the filling with 3 more sheets of buttered phyllo, followed by the remaining filling, then the final 9 sheets of buttered phyllo.

Using a long ruler laid diagonally on top of the pan as a guide, cut the baklava into diamond shapes about 1 inch wide — however, cut only halfway down, leaving the bottom layers intact.

Preheat the oven to 350° F. Bake for about 1½ hours, until the baklava is golden brown on top. Remove from the oven and let sit on a rack for 30 minutes. Pour the cooled syrup evenly over the baklava. After it has cooled completely, finish the cuts. This is best if left to mellow for 24 hours before eating.

BAKED BANANAS IN MAPLE RUM SAUCE

Preparation time: 15 minutes   **Baking time:** 15 minutes   **Yield:** 4 servings

Everyone ought to have several dessert dishes like this in their repertoire — classy, but almost embarrassingly easy to make. If your bananas are large, 3 should be enough here. These could be served plain, but they are much better served on pound cake and topped with ice cream.

4 small to medium-size
  bananas, peeled, halved
  lengthwise, and then
  crosswise
2 tablespoons unsalted butter
⅓ cup maple syrup
¼ cup dark rum
1 tablespoon lemon juice
4 slices pound cake
Vanilla ice cream

Preheat the oven to 375° F. Butter a large, enameled skillet or baking dish and lay the bananas in it, flat side down. Set aside.

Melt the butter in a saucepan, then add the maple syrup. Bring to a boil, boil for a moment, then add the rum and lemon juice. As soon as the syrup returns to a boil, remove from the heat, and pour over the bananas. Place in the oven and bake for 15 minutes, basting once or twice. While the bananas bake, put a piece of pound cake on each dessert plate.

After 15 minutes, remove the bananas from the oven. Using a slotted spatula, transfer several banana slices next to each piece of pound cake. Put the skillet on the burner — or transfer the liquid to a saucepan if you used a casserole — and quickly reduce the liquid to a thick syrup, over high heat. Spoon ice cream over the bananas and pound cake, then top each with plenty of hot sauce.

MAPLE WALNUT ICE CREAM

Preparation time: About 40 minutes   **Yield:** About 1 quart

This is an excellent, basic maple ice cream, good alone or with cake or pie. One thing I love to do with this is to create the Ultimate Death By Chocolate Waffles Experience. You put down a waffle (page 27), mound it with this ice cream, then scoop on tons of fresh sliced strawberries. Besides being a pretty special break-fast, it might replace the cake at your next birthday party.

2 cups light cream
⅔ cup maple syrup
⅓ cup sugar
2 teaspoons vanilla extract
1½ cups heavy cream
½ cup milk
1 cup chopped walnuts
½ teaspoon cinnamon
  (optional)

Gently heat 1 cup of the light cream, the maple syrup, and sugar in a heavy saucepan, just until the sugar is dissolved. Remove from the heat and stir in the vanilla. Pour into a shallow casserole and chill in the freezer until it is very cold. After it has thoroughly chilled, combine it with the remaining 1 cup light cream, heavy cream, and milk in the freezing can of an ice cream maker. Process according to the manufacturer's directions. When it reaches finished consistency, stir in the nuts and cinnamon, if desired. I like to let this firm up in the freezer for several hours, if possible.

MAPLE APPLE ICE

Preparation time: About 35 minutes, plus freezing time   **Yield:** About 8 servings

Here's a refreshing, low-cal way to end a summer's meal on a light maple note. The nice thing about this is there's no ice cream maker involved; you just freeze it in a shallow casserole, and periodically break up the ice crystals with a fork. The ice has the best texture 5 to 7 hours after it is made, though it may be firm enough to eat an hour or so sooner.

Although it essentially defeats the purpose of a low-cal dessert, I like to pour cream over mine. Serve in small, chilled bowls.

2 large, tart apples, peeled,
   cored, and coarsely chopped
2 cups water
½ cup maple syrup
½ cup sugar
¼ cup fresh lemon or
   lime juice
1 teaspoon finely grated
   lemon or lime zest
1 tablespoon minced fresh
   mint (optional)

Combine all the ingredients in a medium-size, noncorroding saucepan. Bring to a boil, cover, and gently simmer for 10 to 15 minutes, until the apples are tender. Remove from the heat and cool for 10 minutes. Working in small batches, puree the mixture in the blender, making sure you get apples and juice in each batch. Transfer the puree to an 8-inch by 8-inch, shallow casserole and cool to room temperature. Place in the freezer compartment of your refrigerator. When the puree is partially frozen around the edges — which could take up to 2 hours — stir with a fork. Cover, and continue to freeze until served, stirring with a fork about every 45 minutes to break up the ice crystals. Mound into chilled bowls and serve, if desired, with a fresh mint leaf garnish.

CANDIED POPCORN AND NUTS

Preparation time: 25 minutes, plus 30 minutes cooling time
Cooking time: 15 minutes   **Yield:** About 2½ quarts

My generation grew up on the mass market version of this, and frankly I don't remember if it was the sweet popcorn or the prize at the bottom of the box we liked more. No matter. This maple version makes a special Christmas gift for the kids — and I use that term loosely — packed into festive bags or tins. Try to enlist the help of a second person to support the pot while you scrape the boiled liquid into the popcorn mix.

2 cups walnuts or other
   nutmeats
1 cup raw (untoasted)
   sunflower seeds
2 quarts popped popcorn,
   unsalted and unbuttered
1½ cups sugar
¾ cup maple syrup
½ cup water
4 tablespoons unsalted butter
½ teaspoon salt
1 teaspoon cinnamon
1 teaspoon vanilla extract

You will need 3 baking sheets for this; grease 2 of them very lightly and set aside. Preheat the oven to 350° F. Spread the nuts and seeds on the third baking sheet. Put the sheet in the preheated oven and toast the nuts and seeds for 7 minutes, stirring once. Turn off the oven. Remove the baking sheet and spread the popcorn on top of the nuts and seeds. Return to the oven to keep warm.

In a heavy-bottomed pot, bring the sugar, maple syrup, water, butter, and salt to a boil. Boil, partially covered, until the mixture reaches 290° F. on a candy thermometer. Remove from the heat and then stir in the cinnamon and vanilla. Quickly transfer the popcorn mix to the largest bowl you have and pour in the hot liquid. Working quickly — it will soon stiffen — stir to coat the entire mixture. Spread on the greased baking sheets and cool for 30 minutes. Break the mixture apart, then store in plastic bags or tins.

Beverages, Butters, & Relishes

From the potable to the spreadable —
a short but sweet compilation

ICED MAPLE-ESPRESSO SHAKE

Preparation time: 5 minutes   **Yield:** 2 servings (or less, depending on your willpower)

If you love coffee and ice cream, this recipe alone may be grounds for leaving me in your will. It is simply addicting. On more than one hot summer's eve, I've been known to skip dinner in favor of a frosty mug of this. It couldn't be quicker to make — just buzz it all in the blender and serve.

3 ice cubes
¾ cup cold, brewed espresso
  or other strong coffee
½ cup milk
¼ cup maple syrup
½ pint good quality vanilla
  ice cream
1 tablespoon coffee liqueur
  (optional)

Chill two big glasses in the freezer. Put the ice cubes inside a folded tea towel and crush them, just a little, with a hammer. In a blender, combine the crushed ice with the remaining ingredients. Process briefly until smooth, but with a slight ice-grainy texture. Pour into the frosted mugs and enjoy.

LEMON AND LIME HERBAL COOLER

Preparation time: 10 minutes   **Yield:** About ½ gallon

I drink gallons of this sort of thing in the summertime. There's a lot of flexibility here, as far as what kind of herb tea you can use. Lemon is probably my favorite, but I've also used orange and raspberry flavored herb tea, and chamomile and peppermint, too. Don't let the tea steep for more than 5 minutes, or you'll overpower the maple flavor.

8 bags lemon or other herb tea
2 quarts boiling hot water
¼ cup fresh lemon juice
¼ cup fresh lime juice
¾ to 1 cup maple syrup
Sprigs of fresh mint,
   if available
Ice

Put the tea bags in a large (not plastic) bowl and pour in the water. Steep for 5 minutes and then remove the tea bags with a slotted spoon. Stir in the remaining ingredients, except the ice, and cool to room temperature. Remove the mint and transfer the liquid to a large jug. Add about 2 cups of ice cubes, cover, and refrigerate if not using right away.

MAPLE AND YOGURT SMOOTHIE

Preparation time: 5 minutes   **Yield:** 2 servings

There are, of course, almost unlimited possibilities for maple smoothies. I've used bananas here, but soft berries in season are also terrific; any soft fruit will work. You can make spiked versions, by adding a compatible spirit or liqueur — Kahlua would be good here, for instance. Let your imagination and taste buds be your guide, bearing in mind the basic proportions of yogurt to maple and fruit.

1 cup plain yogurt
½ cup milk
⅓ cup maple syrup
1 ripe banana, peeled
Pinch cinnamon
Several ice cubes

Combine everything, except the ice, in a blender. Put the ice in the folds of a tea towel and shatter them with a hammer. Add to the blender and process until smooth. It's fine if shards of ice remain after the blending. Serve at once.

ESSENCE OF FALL FRUIT BUTTER

Preparation time: 30 minutes
Cooking and baking time: 2½ hours total   **Yield:** 4 half-pint jars

Here's the best of the fall fruit, distilled into a single fruit butter. Faintly spiced, fairly sweet, this makes a great all-purpose spread for toast, hot crusty biscuits, muffins, and the like. This couldn't be simpler to make: Cook a little fruit, puree it, and put it in the oven.

2 pounds apples, peeled, quartered, and cored
2 pounds ripe pears, peeled, quartered, and cored
1½ cups water
2 tablespoons lemon juice
¾ cup maple syrup
¼ teaspoon cinnamon
¼ teaspoon ground ginger

Cut the apples and pears into chunks — removing any bad spots — and combine them in a large, noncorroding pot. Add the water and lemon juice. Bring to a boil over moderate heat. Cover, reduce the heat to low, and simmer for 30 minutes, stirring occasionally. Remove from the heat. Preheat the oven to 350° F.

Sieve or puree the fruit into a large bowl, adding all the liquid. (I use a Foley food mill; you could use a processor.) Stir in the maple syrup and spices, then transfer to a large glass or enameled casserole. Bake in the oven for 1½ to 2 hours, stirring now and then (especially around the edges), until the puree is reduced by about half. Pack into clean, sterilized jars, seal, and process for 10 minutes in a boiling-water bath. Cool and store. For short-term use, this can be packed into jars and stored in the refrigerator, without processing, for up to 4 weeks.

PINEAPPLE PEACH BUTTER

Preparation time: 45 minutes
Cooking and baking time: About 2½ hours   **Yield:** 4 half-pint jars

Pineapples and peaches, I think, are two fruits that combine especially well with maple, and that's why I like this butter. This makes a nice topping for vanilla ice cream, or it can be stirred into plain yogurt for a quick, intense fruit lift. It's good on pancakes, too.

3 pounds ripe peaches
2 (20-ounce cans) unsweetened, crushed pineapple
½ cup water
¼ cup lemon juice
1 cinnamon stick
½ cup maple syrup

Bring a medium-size pot of water to a boil. Drop in the peaches, several at a time, and let the water come back to a boil. Boil for 15 seconds, then remove the peaches with a slotted spoon. When cool enough to handle, slip off the skins and cut the peach flesh into chunks. Transfer to a large, noncorroding pot and add the pineapple and its juice, water, lemon juice, and cinnamon stick. Bring to a boil over moderate heat. Reduce the heat, cover partially, and simmer gently for 30 minutes, stirring occasionally, until the peaches are very soft. Remove from the heat and take out the cinnamon stick. Preheat the oven to 350° F.

Sieve or puree the fruit, transferring it to a large bowl. Add the maple syrup, stir well, then scrape into a large, noncorroding casserole. Cook in the oven for as long as 2 hours, stirring occasionally, until it is reduced by about half. Pack into clean, sterilized jars, seal, and process for 10 minutes in a boiling-water bath. Cool and store. For short-term storage, this will keep in the refrigerator for a number of weeks, no processing required.

WORLD CLASS MAPLE-BASIL MUSTARD

Preparation time: 25 minutes (plus 2 or more hours to rest)
Cooking time: 15 minutes   **Yield:** About 1½ cups

Not to blow my own horn, but my friend Dan says that his father — who collects mustards from all over the world — says this rivals the best of them. I know I sure like it, and I bet you will, too. It has guts, but with a pleasant, grainy personality. I use it on sandwiches, in salad dressings, marinades — with just about anything that calls for mustard.

⅓ cup yellow mustard seeds
2 tablespoons mustard
  powder (I like Colman's)
½ cup water
⅓ cup apple cider vinegar
⅓ cup maple syrup
¾ teaspoon salt
1 teaspoon dried basil

Put the mustard seeds, mustard powder, and water in a blender and process for 30 to 60 seconds, until the mixture takes on a thick, grainy texture. Scrape into a bowl and let sit, uncovered, for 2 or more hours; this helps release some of the bitter components.

After several hours, return the mixture to the blender along with the remaining ingredients and process until slightly smooth, yet still somewhat grainy. Scrape into a double boiler and cook over simmering water for about 10 minutes, stirring often. Scrape into a bowl and let cool. Taste. It may need a touch of maple, or salt, or vinegar. Pack into a jar with a lid, then refrigerate; it will last indefinitely.

BEET AND PEAR RELISH

Preparation time: 30 minutes   **Yield:** About 2 cups

You can do all sorts of things with this sweet relish. In the summer I like to serve it as is, on a plate with a variety of cold nibbles (try stirring in some fresh, chopped mint). In the cooler months I gently cook the whole shebang in a saucepan with a large handful of cranberries, until the cranberries pop and soften — maybe 10 minutes. This I serve with poultry or pork. Depending on how many cranberries you use, it might need a touch more maple to round off the tart edge. This keeps well in the refrigerator, tightly covered in a jar.

4 medium-size beets,
  simmered until tender
1 firm, ripe pear, peeled
  and diced
⅓ cup chopped raisins
3 tablespoons maple syrup
2 tablespoons fresh lemon
  juice
¼ teaspoon ground ginger
  or about 1 teaspoon minced
  fresh gingerroot
⅛ teaspoon cinnamon

When the beets are cool enough to handle, rub off the skins, then cut the beets into small dices. Combine with the remaining ingredients and stir well. Refrigerate, covered, until serving.

Maple Savories

Some not-too-sweet temptations
from the pan, oven, grill

SPICY SWEET & SOUR SALAD DRESSING

Preparation time: 10 minutes   **Yield:** About 1 cup

Just a little bit of this goes a long way to brighten up a tossed salad with an Oriental accent. And this is the dressing of choice for the Sweet & Sour Chicken Cashew Salad (page 119).

¼ cup vegetable oil
  (part olive is good)
¼ cup apple cider vinegar
¼ cup maple syrup
3 tablespoons tamari or
  soy sauce
1 tablespoon Dijon-style
  mustard
1 garlic clove, minced
⅛ teaspoon cayenne
⅛ teaspoon ginger
⅛ teaspoon cinnamon
⅛ teaspoon ground cloves
¼ teaspoon finely grated
  orange zest

Combine all of the ingredients in a mixing bowl and whisk thoroughly. Taste and correct the precise balance of ingredients to your liking, adding a bit more vinegar, maple syrup, or spice, if you like. Transfer to a bottle, cap, and refrigerate. Shake well before using.

LEMON BASIL SALAD DRESSING

Preparation time: 5 minutes   **Yield:** About 1 cup

Somebody could bottle this and make a fortune, that's how good it is. And very versatile. I use it on green salads, 3-bean salads, and green bean salads (see page 116).

⅓ cup vegetable oil
  (may be part olive)
¼ cup apple cider vinegar
¼ cup maple syrup
1 tablespoon Dijon-style
  mustard
Pinch salt and pepper
½ teaspoon crushed dried
  basil (more if fresh)
Pinch finely grated lemon zest

Whisk together all the ingredients in a bowl. Taste and adjust the flavor with a little more maple or vinegar, if needed. Bottle and refrigerate.

Creamy Lemon Basil Dressing
Prepare the dressing as above. Whisk in ½ to ¾ cup sour cream.

CUCUMBER & APPLE SALAD

Preparation time: 20 minutes, plus at least 1½ hours to refrigerate   **Yield:** 4 to 6 servings

Call this a salad, or relish, or raita — the yogurt-based Indian dish it is modeled after. What it is, is a cool, refreshing counterpoint to hot curries, though it could be served with any number of savory foods. There's an agreeable balance of sweet and sharp flavors, with the maple sounding a soft, background note. A pinch of chopped fresh mint really makes this shine, if you happen to have some on hand.

1 large cucumber, peeled, halved, and seeded
¼ teaspoon salt
1¼ cups plain yogurt
1½ tablespoons maple syrup
1 tablespoon minced onion
½ teaspoon finely grated orange zest
1 tart, firm apple, peeled, quartered, and cored

Chop the cucumber into uniform, small dices and transfer to a small bowl. Stir in the salt and set aside for 30 minutes.

Stir together the yogurt, maple syrup, onion, and orange zest. Chop the apple into uniform, small dices and stir into the yogurt. Cover and refrigerate.

After the 30 minutes have elapsed, squeeze the excess moisture out of the cucumber with your hands. Fold the cukes into the yogurt mixture. Chill for at least 1 hour, preferably more, before serving.

LEMON BASIL GREEN BEAN SALAD

Preparation time: 15 minutes   **Yield:** 4 servings

Cool, crisp, colorful — and likely to become one of your most requested summer salads. It is best if the salad is left for at least an hour in the refrigerator before it is served.

3 cups fresh green beans, ends pinched off, and broken in half
½ cup Lemon Basil Salad Dressing (page 114)
1 small red onion, halved and thinly sliced
½ cup finely chopped red bell pepper
1 celery rib, finely chopped
1 tablespoon capers (optional, but highly recommended)
Salt and pepper

Bring 2 quarts of salted water to a boil in a large pot. Add the beans and boil them, about 6 to 8 minutes, just until tender. Drain and transfer to a bowl. Immediately stir in the dressing, followed by the remaining ingredients, adding salt and pepper to taste. Then cool thoroughly. Cover and refrigerate for at least 1 hour before serving.

ROASTED PEPPER & CHICK-PEA SALAD

Preparation time: 30 minutes   **Yield:** 4 to 5 servings

There was a time when I wouldn't bother with roasting peppers. When I actually did try it though, I was amazed what a difference the roasting made in flavor and texture. In the summer, I like to roast peppers right on a hot grill; in other seasons, right on top of the burner grid on my gas stove. You can also broil peppers in a shallow pan in any oven. The flavors of this salad hit just the nicest harmony. Do use smoked cheddar — it makes a difference with the maple in there. This is wonderful with grilled foods.

¼ cup vegetable oil
2 tablespoons lemon juice
2 tablespoons maple syrup
1½ tablespoons Dijon-style
  mustard
3 large green or red bell
  peppers
2 cups cooked chick-peas
2 tablespoons minced onion
½ cup diced smoked cheddar
  cheese
½ cup diced ham
Salt and pepper

Make the dressing by whisking together the oil, lemon juice, maple syrup, and mustard. Set aside.

Roast the peppers on a grill, over a hot burner, or under a broiler, turning often with tongs, to char the entire surface. Put them into a plastic bag, twist shut, and freeze for 15 minutes — this will steam off the skins. Remove from the freezer, cut out the stem end, drain, and halve them. Remove the seeds and skins; the skins should peel right off. Slice the peppers into narrow strips.

Toss the peppers into the dressing along with the chick-peas, onion, cheese, and ham. Stir. Chill for several hours. Season to taste with salt and pepper before serving.

SALAD OF JÍCAMA, GRAPES, & ORANGE

Preparation time: 15 minutes   **Yield:** 4 to 5 servings

Jícama (HEE-ka-ma) is one of those "new" vegetables we've been seeing in the markets lately. It looks something like a flattish potato, comes in a whole range of sizes, and is imported to this country from Mexico. Plain, it's a trifle drab, but it has a crisp, crunchy texture, and it perks right up in raw salads of this sort. Do let the salad sit in the refrigerator for a couple of hours before serving; it really helps the character of the jícama to bathe in the acid juices.

1 small jícama
3 tablespoons lime juice
2½ tablespoons maple syrup
1 tablespoon vegetable oil
Pinch salt
1 orange
½ cup green seedless grapes, halved
2 tablespoons minced red onion

Cut the jícama lengthwise into ¼-inch slabs and peel with a paring knife. Cut the slabs in ¼-inch-wide sticks, then gather the sticks and slice them so you end up with ¼-inch dices. Put 1½ to 2 cups in a mixing bowl. Pour the lime juice, maple syrup, and oil over the jícama and toss. Stir in the salt.

Halve the orange, remove any seeds, then free the sections with a knife. Squeeze them and their juices into the bowl, then add the grapes and onion. Cover and refrigerate for several hours before serving, stirring once or twice.

SWEET & SOUR CHICKEN CASHEW SALAD

Preparation time: 20 minutes, plus time to cook the chicken   **Yield:** 4 to 5 servings

This is not so much the sort of chicken salad you'd put in a sandwich as it is something you'd arrange in the middle of a colorful plate of greens and serve for a light lunch or dinner. There are all sorts of contrasting flavors and textures here, much to the salad's advantage.

The tahini specified below is a sesame seed paste, widely available in health food stores. Another way to make this is to skip the tahini, and substitute about a tablespoon of Dijon-style mustard.

½ cup Spicy Sweet & Sour
  Salad Dressing (page 113)
2 tablespoons tahini
2 cups bite-size chunks cooked
  chicken
1 celery rib, finely chopped
2 scallions, thinly sliced
½ cup coarsely chopped
  cashews
1 tablespoon minced jalapeño
  peppers (optional)
Lemon juice
Salt and pepper to taste
Greens
Minced raisins (for garnish)

Put the salad dressing into a bowl and thoroughly whisk in the tahini so the mixture thickens a little. Fold in the chicken, celery, scallions, cashews, and peppers, if you are using them. Give it a little squeeze of lemon and then taste and correct the seasonings to your liking. Cover and refrigerate until serving. Serve on a plate of greens, garnished very lightly — if desired — with the raisins.

SWEET POTATO, BACON, & MAPLE BISQUE

Preparation time: 40 minutes   **Yield:** 4 to 6 servings

What a wonderful, cold weather soup this is! The maple lifts the sweetness and flavor of the sweet potatoes, while the bacon and onion add depth and contrast. Excellent with cornbread or corn muffins and a mixed green salad served with a mustardy viniagrette. This can also be made with ham instead of bacon, in which case you would simply sauté the onion in some butter.

4 cups peeled, diced sweet potatoes
4 cups water
6 bacon slices
1 small onion, minced
1½ cups light cream or milk
1 teaspoon salt or more to taste
¼ cup maple syrup
¼ teaspoon cinnamon

Combine the sweet potatoes and water in a large, heavy-bottomed soup pot. Bring to a boil, cover, and reduce the heat to a simmer. Cook for about 20 minutes, until the potatoes are very tender. Remove from the heat.

While the potatoes are cooking, fry the bacon in a skillet until crisp. Remove from the pan and blot with paper towels. Pour out all but about 3 tablespoons of the fat, then add the onion and sauté for 5 minutes. Remove from the heat.

Working in batches, puree the potatoes and cooking water in a blender or food processor. (Always be careful when pureeing hot liquids in the blender. Never fill the container more than one-third full to avoid the risk of the lid blowing off.) Return the puree to the soup pot, then stir in the onion, light cream or milk, salt, maple syrup, and cinnamon. Crumble the bacon into bits and add that also. Heat, but do not boil, and serve piping hot. Put a small dollop of sour cream in each bowl, if that sounds good.

RICHARD'S CHICKEN WITH MAPLE-MUSTARD GLAZE

Preparation time: 20 minutes, plus 30 to 60 minutes to rest
Cooking time: 20 to 30 minutes   **Yield:** 4 servings

This recipe is an adaptation of one developed by my friend Richard Sax, a gifted cook, food writer, and all-around fine person. What he does is make the sauce, minus the mustard, and brush it on the chicken. Then he broils the chicken 6 inches from the heat, 15 minutes on each side, and brushes the mustard on at the last minute. Here's my way, for the grill, but you could also broil it Richard's way.

1 broiler-fryer chicken, cut up
¼ cup maple syrup
3 tablespoons Dijon-style
   mustard
2 teaspoons tamari or
   soy sauce
1 tablespoon lemon juice
1 garlic clove, minced
½ teaspoon ground pepper

Trim the excess fat from the chicken. Wash the pieces and blot them dry with paper towels. Set aside. Combine the remaining ingredients in a saucepan and bring to a boil, boiling for 1 minute. Remove from the heat. Place the chicken in a large, shallow casserole and brush on both sides with half the maple sauce. Set aside for 30 to 60 minutes. Grill, on a hot grill, periodically basting the pieces with leftover sauce, until the chicken is done.

ORANGE-SPICED CHICKEN WINGS

Preparation time: 15 minutes, plus 24 hours to marinate
Cooking time: 15 to 20 minutes   **Yield:** 4 servings

Soaking chicken wings in this buttermilk-orange-maple bath makes the meat butter-tender and infuses it with a sweet essence. The flavor here is delicate and subtle, so don't serve this with anything overpowering. A simple grain pilaf, perhaps even slightly curried, would be just fine.

1½ cups buttermilk
⅓ cup maple syrup
2 oranges, halved, and
  sections cut out
1 teaspoon cinnamon
16 to 20 chicken wings

Mix the buttermilk and maple syrup in a large bowl. Briefly process the orange sections and cinnamon in a blender to make a coarse puree. Stir the orange mixture into the buttermilk, then add the chicken wings. Stir to coat. Cover and refrigerate for at least 1 hour or up to 24 hours, stirring every now and then. Grill or broil, far enough from the heat to prevent excessive charring. Turn from time to time, brushing with some of the buttermilk marinade.

THE MAPLE SYRUP COOKBOOK

TANGY NORTH COUNTRY BASTING SAUCE

Preparation time: 10 minutes   **Cooking time:** 10 minutes   **Yield:** About 3 cups

This barbecue sauce, though not faithful to any particular school of barbecue sauce thought, is versatile, spicy, and no slouch in the flavor department. It's tops on barbecued or broiled chicken. One thing I like to do with it is combine it with hot peppers, more spices, and onions for the Hot & Spicy Shrimp & Sausage Kabobs (page 124).

1 cup catsup
⅔ cup apple cider vinegar
½ cup vegetable oil
½ cup maple syrup
1 tablespoon Worcestershire
  sauce
1 tablespoon Dijon-style
  mustard
½ teaspoon chili powder
½ teaspoon salt
¼ teaspoon cayenne pepper

In a small saucepan, bring all the ingredients to a boil over medium heat, stirring occasionally. Reduce the heat and cook gently for 10 minutes, stirring from time to time. Cool, then store in a covered jar in the refrigerator. This will keep for at least 4 weeks in the refrigerator in a tightly covered jar.

HOT & SPICY SHRIMP & SAUSAGE KABOBS

Preparation time: 20 minutes, plus at least 1 hour to marinate
Cooking time: About 10 minutes   **Yield:** 4 servings

Whether or not you agree with my friend Cindy — who called this the best meal of her entire life (she had a sheltered childhood) — I do think you'll be pleased. The heat can be regulated here by gauging the amount and type of chili peppers you use; for most folks, I find the 2 tablespoons of jalapeños sufficient. Of course, if you have a stash of fresh, hot peppers you fancy, then use them instead. Good beer drinking grub this is.

1¼ cups Tangy North Country Basting Sauce (page 123)
1½ tablespoons lemon juice
2 tablespoons minced onion
2 tablespoons minced jalapeño peppers, canned or fresh
1 pound chorizo or linguica sausage
1 pound fresh large shrimp in the shell

Blend the basting sauce, lemon juice, onion, and jalapeño peppers in a large bowl. Set aside.

Bring 2 quarts of water to a boil in a large pot. Prick the sausage several times with a fork and then boil for 5 minutes. When cool enough to handle, cut into ½-inch slices and add to the marinade along with the shrimp. Stir to coat everything. Cover and set aside for 1 hour; it may be refrigerated for several hours.

Thread 4 or 5 long skewers alternately with the shrimp and sausage. Either grill or broil, far enough from the heat to prevent charring. Turn occasionally, brushing with more sauce. The total cooking time should be around 10 minutes; test one of the shrimp to see if they are done. And be sure to tell your guests that the shrimp is in the shell.

HAM STEAKS IN RUM RAISIN SAUCE

Preparation time: 15 minutes   **Cooking time:** About 1 hour   **Yield:** 2 to 3 servings

Here's a simple, tasty way to prepare ham steaks. Try this with biscuits and Bacon Braised Onions (page 118).

1 pound ham steak
1 cup apple cider
¼ cup plus 2 tablespoons
   maple syrup
¼ cup dark rum
2 to 3 tablespoons orange
   juice, preferably fresh
½ cup raisins

Preheat the oven to 350° F. Put the ham steak in a shallow casserole slightly larger than the steak. Set aside. Bring the cider, ¼ cup of the maple syrup, the rum, orange juice, and raisins to a near boil in a small saucepan. Cover and let sit for 10 minutes. Remove the raisins with a slotted spoon, put them in a small bowl, and spoon enough of the hot liquid over them to cover completely. Pour the remaining liquid over the ham and bake for 1 hour.

When the hour is up, combine the raisins and their soaking liquid in a blender with several tablespoons of the casserole juice and the remaining 2 tablespoons maple syrup. Process briefly —a little roughness is good — and pour it directly over the ham. Run the ham under the broiler for just a few moments, until it sizzles and browns; keep a close eye on it. Serve hot.

OPAL'S HAM LOAF WITH MAPLE GLAZE

Preparation time: 15 minutes
Baking time: 1¼ hours   **Yield:** 2 large loaves, about 8 servings per loaf

Opal is my mother-in-law, a wonderful woman whose cooking talents are known far and wide around Oregon, Ohio. This is her recipe for ham loaf, which can be served at breakfast, lunch, or dinner — hot or cold. For breakfast I like to heat slices in butter and serve with waffles or eggs and biscuits. The glaze can go on as the loaf bakes — which imbues it with a lovely maple essence — or it can be spooned on individual slices when served. This is a large recipe, but one loaf can be frozen for later.

Ham Loaf
1½ pounds ground smoked ham (ask your butcher to do this)
1½ pounds lean ground pork
1 cup fine, dry bread crumbs
4 large eggs, lightly beaten
1 cup milk

Maple Glaze
¾ cup maple syrup
¼ cup apple cider vinegar
1 teaspoon dry mustard
Pinch cloves

Preheat the oven to 375° F. Mix the ham, pork, and bread crumbs in a large mixing bowl. Add the eggs and milk and mix thoroughly. Divide between two large ungreased nonaluminum loaf pans and shape the tops so they're somewhat rounded. Place the loaves in the oven.

To make the glaze, combine the maple syrup, vinegar, mustard, and cloves in a small saucepan. Bring to a boil.

If you plan to pour the glaze over the ham loaf as it bakes, boil briefly, perhaps a minute or two, because it will cook further and thicken in the oven. But if you want to serve it on the side, boil it several minutes longer, so you end up with a thicker glaze.

To bake without the glaze, bake the loaf for 1¼ hours, carefully pouring off the juices when done. Serve with the hot glaze on the side.

To bake with the glaze, after 45 minutes of baking, pour the juices off the loaf and pour on the hot glaze, using half the glaze recipe per loaf. Bake for another 30 minutes, basting with the glaze periodically (tilt the pan so the basting juices run to one end). Serve hot or cool in the pan.

MAPLE BAKED BEANS

Preparation time: 25 minutes, plus at least 1 hour soaking time
Cooking time: 1½ to 2 hours   **Baking time:** 2½ to 3½ hours   **Yield:** About 6 servings

Baked beans, like chili, is one of those dishes that ignites controversy. Almost every variable — what type of beans to use, choice of seasonings and sweetener, salt pork or not — has its own special lobbying group. And so, at the risk of adding fuel to the fire, here is my own favorite maple version.

1 pound navy or pea beans
⅓ cup vegetable oil
1 cup chopped onions
1 green bell pepper, chopped
1 celery rib, chopped
2 to 3 garlic cloves, minced
½ cup maple syrup
½ cup tomato puree or
    crushed tomatoes
2 tablespoons blackstrap
    molasses
2 tablespoons apple cider
    vinegar
1 tablespoon Dijon-style
    mustard
1½ teaspoons salt
¼ teaspoon pepper
1 bay leaf
¼ cup chopped fresh parsley

Pick the beans over, removing any rubble such as sticks and pebbles. Rinse them well, then place in a large bowl with plenty of hot water. Let soak for at least 1 hour, or as long as overnight. Drain, then combine the beans with about 4 quarts fresh hot water in a large pot. Bring to a boil, reduce the heat, and simmer, partially covered, just until tender — 1½ to 2 hours. Drain, reserving the cooking water.

While the beans cook, heat the oil in a large skillet. Add the onion, pepper, and celery, and sauté for several minutes, adding the garlic at the end. Remove from the heat and set aside. Preheat the oven to 325° F.

Whisk together the remaining ingredients, adding 1 cup of the reserved cooking water. Combine the beans, sautéed vegetables, and tomato-maple mixture in a large bowl. Mix well. Turn the beans into a large, shallow casserole and cover tightly with foil. Bake for 2½ to 3½ hours. Check periodically to make sure they have enough liquid, adding more of the cooking water, if necessary.

WINTER SQUASH SPOONBREAD

Preparation time: 35 to 40 minutes   **Baking time:** About 35 minutes   **Yield:** 8 servings

Spoonbread is somewhere between a soufflé and cornbread, based on a thick sauce known as a rick. Here, I put pureed winter squash — acorn, butternut, or even pumpkin — into the rick with a little maple syrup. This puffs up nicely, but doesn't stay that way long, once it comes out of the oven. It is very good with poultry dishes. I often serve leftovers, cold, for breakfast, with a little cream and maple drizzled over it.

1½ cups peeled and diced winter squash, (½-inch pieces)
⅓ cup maple syrup
2 cups milk
1 cup cornmeal, preferably stone-ground
¾ teaspoon salt
⅛ teaspoon nutmeg
4 tablespoons unsalted butter, cut into ½-inch pieces
5 large eggs, separated

Preheat the oven to 375° F. Butter a large, shallow casserole and reserve. Put the squash into a large saucepan with plenty of water. Bring to a boil, cover, then simmer for about 20 minutes, until the squash is very soft. Drain in a colander for several minutes, then puree the squash in a blender with the maple syrup. Set aside.

Put the milk in a large, heavy-bottomed pot. While the milk is still cool, gradually whisk in the cornmeal. Turn the heat to medium-high and cook the cornmeal, stirring, until it starts to thicken, about 3 to 5 minutes. Reduce the heat slightly and continue to stir and cook for several more minutes, until it is quite thick. Stir in the salt, nutmeg, butter, and pureed mixture and whisk until smooth. Remove from the heat and whisk in the egg yolks. Pour into a large mixing bowl.

Beat the egg whites until stiff, then fold them into the cooked mixture. Pour into prepared pan and bake for about 35 minutes, until golden and puffed; large cracks will appear on the surface. Serve hot or very warm.

BAKED STUFFED SWEET POTATOES

Preparation time: 20 minutes, plus cooling time
Baking time: 70 to 85 minutes total   **Yield:** 4 servings

Here's an easy, fun recipe, and a nice switch from candied sweet potatoes. I always bake up several extra potatoes for the filling, otherwise when the skins are stuffed, they come out looking somewhat flat and undernourished.

4 medium-size sweet potatoes
   (about 2½ pounds)
¼ cup sour cream
¼ cup maple syrup
1 tablespoon butter
¼ teaspoon salt
Pinch cinnamon
Pinch nutmeg
Pinch ground cloves
Brown sugar (optional)

Preheat the oven to 400° F. Prick the potatoes with a fork, once each, and place them on a baking sheet. Bake for 50 to 60 minutes, until the insides are done. Remove from the oven and set aside until they are cool enough to handle.

Halve the sweet potatoes lengthwise, carefully scoop out the insides, and reserve the shells. Combine the insides in a mixing bowl with the remaining ingredients. Whip with an electric mixer until smooth. Pack the 4 best shells with the filling, mounding it in. Place close together in a pie pan or small casserole. Sprinkle the tops, if desired, with a touch of brown sugar. Bake for 20 to 25 minutes, until heated through.

BACON BRAISED ONIONS

Preparation time: About 30 minutes   **Yield:** 4 to 5 servings

I've really tried to like whole onions in the past, but never really cared for any of the recipes I found. Until this one. This is nothing less than a sensational way to do up boiling onions to serve with roasts, steak, and other meats. What you do is briefly sauté the onions in bacon fat, add water and seasonings, then cover and braise. Then you finish them with a touch of maple and sprinkle on the bacon. Better to choose the medium-small boiling onions than the tiny ones — saves work in peeling.

1 pound medium-small boiling
   onions
3 bacon slices
½ cup water
1 teaspoon soy sauce
1 bay leaf
¼ teaspoon dried thyme
2 tablespoons maple syrup

Peel the onions and cut off the very (hairy) end part at the root end. Make a shallow little *x* in the root end, to encourage even cooking. Set aside.

Fry the bacon until crisp in a heavy skillet. Remove the bacon, blot with paper towels, and set aside. Add the onions to the fat and stir to coat. Cook over medium heat, partially covered, for 5 minutes, stirring occasionally. Stir in the water, soy sauce, bay leaf, and thyme. Cover, reduce the heat slightly, and braise for 10 to 15 minutes, until the onions are almost tender all the way through. The exact cooking time will depend on the size of the onions. Stir the maple syrup into the pan — which should still have a thin layer of liquid in it — and turn up the heat. Cook and stir, until the liquid turns to a syrupy glaze; it shouldn't take long. Crumble the bacon and stir it in. Serve hot, spooning on any available glaze.

Index